Clean Transport

The Legal Framework for Achieving Net Zero

Editor
William Smith

Managing director
Sian O'Neill

Clean Transport: The Legal Framework for Achieving Net Zero
is published by

Globe Law and Business Ltd
3 Mylor Close
Horsell
Woking
Surrey GU21 4DD
United Kingdom
Tel: +44 20 3745 4770
www.globelawandbusiness.com

Printed and bound by 4Edge Ltd, Hockley, Essex

Clean Transport: The Legal Framework for Achieving Net Zero

ISBN 9781837230150
EPUB ISBN 9781837230167
Adobe PDF ISBN 9781837230174

Table of contents

Foreword ... 7
Richard Marshall
DWS Infrastructure

I. Decarbonising the transport sector ... 9
Ellie Gilbert
Anna Sweeney
Addleshaw Goddard

1. Introduction ... 9
2. International decarbonisation strategies ... 10
3. The UK's approach to decarbonisation ... 12
4. Early days of government climate action ... 13
5. Climate Change Act 2008 ... 14
6. Carbon budgets and carbon targets ... 14
7. Transport and meeting the UK's climate targets ... 16
8. Road to Zero Strategy ... 17
9. The UK's Ten Point Plan for a Green Industrial Revolution ... 18
10. The UK's transport decarbonisation plan ... 21
11. UK Hydrogen Strategy ... 23
12. Net Zero Strategy: Build Back Greener and Powering Up Britain: Net Zero Growth Plan ... 23

13. Electric vehicle infrastructure strategy 24
14. Carbon Budget Delivery Plan and ZEV Mandate 24
15. The UK general election 2024 24
16. Middle East approach to decarbonisation 25
17. Conclusion 27

II. Rail decarbonisation 29
Martin Fleetwood
Ross Sandford
Rachel Scott
Addleshaw Goddard

1. The legal imperative: United Kingdom 29
2. Technology: "What does the future look like?" 35
3. How do we get there? 45
4. Reducing carbon in the supporting infrastructure for new power systems 50
5. Conclusion 56

III. Zero and low emission road vehicles 59
Ellen Beardsworth
Paul Dight
Anna Sweeney
Addleshaw Goddard

1. Zero emission road vehicles 59
2. Zero emission technology options 59
3. Impactful use cases 68
4. The legal imperative: the Zero Emission Vehicle Mandate 70
5. Challenges faced by the automotive industry 71
6. How is the market responding to the challenges? 78
7. Conclusion: why could zero emission vehicles be helpful to reaching net zero target? 87

IV. Public transport and payments 89
Jack Houselander
Euan Towers
Addleshaw Goddard

1. Introduction 89
2. Payment services: the legal and compliance context 90
3. The payment service provider relationship 94
4. How does a payment transaction work? 94
5. 'Open loop' and 'closed loop' payments in transport 98
6. Models 103

V. Connected autonomous vehicles: the future of mobility and their role in achieving net zero 107
Charles Christie
Nathalie Moreno
William Smith
Addleshaw Goddard

1. Introduction 107
2. Understanding connected autonomous vehicles 107
3. Self-driving and levels of automation 108
4. Benefits of connected autonomous vehicles 108
5. Connected autonomous vehicles and net zero 110
6. Legal imperative and the current regulatory landscape 112
7. How do we get there? 115
8. The direction of travel across the globe 118
9. Conclusion 143

VI. Green shipping 145
Ed Watt
Addleshaw Goddard

1. Introduction: the fuel choice dilemma 145
2. International Maritime Organization 147
3. UK measures 148
4. Emissions trading schemes 150
5. Low emission technologies 151
6. Conclusion 161

VII. Aviation and the jet zero ambition 163
Anna Ai
Sophie Black
Sheyda Rimmer
Addleshaw Goddard

1. Introduction 163
2. Legal, political and regulatory background to sustainable aviation 164
3. What does the future look like for the aviation industry? 172
4. Conclusion 179

Addendum 183

About the authors 185

About Globe Law and Business 191

Foreword

Richard Marshall
DWS Infrastructure

When it comes to decarbonisation and the energy transition or, more broadly, sustainability, there is an increasing associated urgency with which investments are needed. The Net Zero by 2050 targets and the long-term temperature goals set out in the Paris Agreement of 2016 started as somewhat distant requirements – achievable given their far-off deadline. However, as the global economy has recovered following the COVID-19 pandemic and emissions reporting requirements across a range of jurisdictions have begun to solidify, the levels of additional action needed to achieve these goals have become starker.

Looking across economic sectors, good progress has been made in many European markets with regard to the decarbonisation of electricity production and, with the de-risking and scaling of wind and solar technologies, capital has flowed into the market. Conversely, transportation has significantly further to go on its decarbonisation journey, despite the high-profile growth of the electric vehicle (EV) market. While many technologies for decarbonising land, sea and air transportation now exist, the challenge for investors is matching the urgency with which capital is needed to scale the deployment of such solutions, with their ultimate fiduciary responsibility to manage risk and return.

It is in this context – the need to balance risk and return, and meeting climate commitments – that navigating and operating within the legal frameworks crafted by governments is a fundamental necessity. It is only with a deep understanding and trust of the regulatory frameworks governing the decarbonisation of the vehicles, trains, aircraft, ships and – crucially – fuels within the clean transportation market that investors will feel the comfort necessary to deploy capital at the scale needed to meet our net zero commitments.

Governments will change and with them the laws they implement, so as with any transition period the shift to low-carbon alternatives will not be straightforward. However, as was seen within the renewable energy market, where immature technologies and small markets have grown to where they are today, with clarity, patience and long-term perspectives on legal frameworks, it can be achieved. Momentum is certainly on the side of clean transport sectors, with the policy responses since the pandemic supply chain disruptions and the European energy crisis meaning the legal tailwinds have never been stronger.

Richard Marshall is the head of infrastructure research at DWS, a diversified global asset manager. Richard is responsible for supporting the DWS infrastructure private equity and debt platforms with actionable investment strategies and approaches to infrastructure portfolio construction.

I. Decarbonising the transport sector

Ellie Gilbert
Anna Sweeney
Addleshaw Goddard

1. Introduction

The transport sector plays a pivotal role in the global economy, enabling the movement of people and goods around the world. However, it is also a major contributor to global carbon emissions, a key driver of climate change. According to the International Energy Agency (IEA), in 2019, the transport sector was responsible for approximately 24% of direct carbon dioxide (CO2) emissions from fuel combustion.[1] Road vehicles (cars, trucks, buses and two- and three-wheelers) accounted for nearly three-quarters of transport CO2 emissions, with the remainder stemming from other modes of transport such as aviation, maritime and rail.

The urgency of decarbonising the transport sector cannot be overstated. As the world grapples with the dual challenges of mitigating climate change and ensuring sustainable economic development, the transition towards a cleaner, greener transport system is of paramount importance.

As this chapter will explore, there is an increasingly complex and ever-changing framework of regulation, policies, reports, targets and ambitions from a number of international, national and industry bodies across the transport sector to reduce the impact that transport has on climate change.

Later chapters in this Special Report will delve deeper into each form of transport and the respective sector decarbonisation strategy (or strategies), critically analysing its progress and identifying areas for improvement. It will assess the implementation and effectiveness of key initiatives that include the use of hydrogen, rail, electric vehicles (EVs), modal shift, connected autonomous vehicles (CAVs), shipping and sustainable aviation fuels (SAFs). By comparing the United Kingdom's efforts to those of other countries, we can glean valuable insights, helping pave the way for a cleaner, greener and more sustainable future of transport.

2. International decarbonisation strategies

The challenge of climate change is a global one and this section explores the key international laws, agreements and initiatives that are shaping the world's approach to reducing carbon emissions. The most significant pieces of global commitments to decarbonisation are as follows.

2.1 United Nations Framework Convention on Climate Change

The United Nations Framework Convention on Climate Change (UNFCCC) is an international treaty aimed at addressing climate change. It was adopted in 1992 and brings together countries to work towards stabilising greenhouse gas (GHG) concentrations in the atmosphere. The treaty established the Conference of the Parties

The UNFCCC plays a crucial role in uniting countries and addressing the issue of climate change on a global scale.

(COP) as the main decision-making authority. COP meetings assess progress and negotiate binding obligations, such as the Paris Agreement. The UNFCCC plays a crucial role in uniting countries and addressing the issue of climate change on a global scale. After the first Intergovernmental Panel on Climate Change (IPCC) report was published in 1990[2] (which underlined the importance of climate change, citing it as a global challenge with potentially significant impacts across the planet) the UN began negotiations on an international treaty, which was the UNFCCC.

The UNFCCC entered into force on 21 March 1994 and, to date, has 198 parties, ranging from Georgia to Nauru to Pakistan. The key objective of the UNFCCC is set out in Article 2: "the stabilisation of greenhouse gases in the atmosphere at a level that would prevent dangerous anthropogenic interference with the climate system".

Parties who have joined the UNFCCC meet at the annual COP with the aim to review progress, negotiate and agree responses to climate change. The first COP was held in Berlin in 1995, and in 2024 COP29 will be held in Azerbaijan.

2.2 Kyoto Protocol

This international treaty, adopted in 1997, legally binds developed countries to emission reduction targets. The Protocol's first commitment period started in 2008 and ended in 2012. The second commitment period began in 2013 and ended in 2020. The Kyoto Protocol was one of the first pieces of international legislation to cover climate change. A total of 84 countries signed the agreement back in 1997 and 46 ratified it. The Kyoto Protocol operates on the principle of 'cap and trade', setting a maximum emission limit for each participating country. Countries that emit less than their quota can sell their surplus allowances to countries that exceed their limit, creating a financial incentive for nations to reduce their GHG emissions. It was the first international agreement to set emission reduction targets.

Annex B sets out binding emission reduction targets for 37 industrialised countries and economies in transition, including the UK, Australia, Japan, Russia and a number of European countries.[3] The Kyoto Protocol has been effectively replaced by the Paris Agreement.

2.3 Paris Agreement

Adopted in 2015 (at COP21), the Paris Agreement sets out a global framework to avoid dangerous climate change by limiting global warming to well below 2°C and pursuing efforts to limit it to 1.5°C. It also aims to strengthen the ability of countries to deal with the impacts of climate change and support them in their efforts to reduce carbon emissions.

To date, the European Union and 194 countries have adopted the Paris Agreement, totalling over 98% of total global GHG emissions. These include Rwanda, Qatar and the People's Republic of Korea (North Korea). The Holy See, Nicaragua and Syria have signed but not ratified the Paris Agreement and Iran, Libya and Yemen have ratified but not signed the Paris Agreement.[4]

Article 6 of the Paris Agreement recognises the role of voluntary cooperation and carbon markets in achieving its goals. Carbon markets have emerged over the past two decades as key tools in the global effort to reduce GHG emissions and combat climate change. They operate on the principle of 'cap and trade', providing economic incentives for reducing emissions.

2.4 Montreal Protocol

Although primarily aimed at protecting the ozone layer by phasing out the production of numerous substances responsible for ozone depletion, it has also contributed significantly to the reduction of GHG emissions. Signed in 1987 by 197 countries, it was the first UN treaty to receive universal ratification.

3. The UK's approach to decarbonisation

In the UK, the transport sector contributed approximately a third of all carbon emissions in 2022 and 91% of this was attributable to road transport.

While this Special Report provides an overview of the UK's approach to decarbonisation, it should be noted that there is a rapidly changing political environment within the UK. Following the outcome of the general election in July 2024 which resulted in a change from a Conservative to a Labour government, it is expected that there will be a period of upheaval across UK government strategy and priorities which will lead to changes in policy, regulation and legislation in and around the transport sector.

Sections 4 to 14 below discuss the UK's historical and current approach to decarbonisation against this backdrop of political uncertainty.

When we talk about 'the government' throughout this chapter, and in this Special Report generally, we are referring to the political party and the individuals that form the government of the UK at any given time. This will not always be the newly elected Labour government led by Kier Starmer, as is the case at the time of writing. We may also specifically mention a devolved government; in which case, we will specify which devolved government we are talking about.

Following the outcome of the general election in July 2024 which resulted in a change from a Conservative to a Labour government, it is expected that there will be a period of upheaval across UK government strategy and priorities which will lead to changes in policy, regulation and legislation in and around the transport sector.

4. Early days of government climate action

The Kyoto Protocol was adopted by the UK in 1997 but entered into force in 2005. In its Annex B, it set emission reduction targets for certain countries, including the UK.

In 2006, the UK's first Climate Change Programme was published. This report detailed how the UK could reach the target set under the Kyoto Protocol to cut GHG emissions by 12.5% and the UK's own first climate target of reducing CO2 emissions by 20% by 2010 (compared to 1990).[5]

The Climate Change and Sustainable Energy Act 2006 introduced a requirement that the Secretary of State for Environment, Food and Rural Affairs would report to parliament on an annual basis on GHG emissions in the UK and what action was being taken by the government to reduce those emissions. The first report was published in July 2007 and covered several early policies and measures in respect of transport such as the Renewable Transport Fuel Obligation, which is an obligation on suppliers of fossil fuels (petrol and diesel) to supply a certain percentage of renewable fuel to the UK market. We discuss this more in Chapter III.

5. Climate Change Act 2008

The more significant changes to the government's approach to climate change and decarbonisation came in the form of the Climate Change Act 2008 and the formation of the UK's Climate Change Committee (CCC).

The CCC is a cross-party, non-departmental public body set up to advise the current government, parliament, devolved legislatures and each of their successors. It became a statutory committee on 1 December 2008 when the Climate Change Act 2008 became law.

The CCC is required by law to provide advice and recommendations to the government on GHG emission reduction targets for 2050,[6] on carbon budgets[7] and any other assistance on request from the secretary of state.[8] The CCC must also report on its progress under the Climate Change Act 2008[9] and has provided annual progress reports to parliament every year since 2009.[10]

Notably, the CCC, as an independent advisory body, helps to preserve impartiality and consistency, shield climate promises from being changed by governments on a political whim and maintain focus on the UK's climate commitments across successive legislatures.

Chris Stark, the previous chief executive of the CCC, has been appointed by Ed Miliband, the Secretary of State for Energy Security and Net Zero to lead a new "control centre to turbocharge the government's mission to provide Britain with cheaper and clean power by 2030".[11]

6. Carbon budgets and carbon targets

The UK was the first major economy to set legally binding carbon targets, enforced by setting carbon budgets, over 15 years ago.

A carbon target is a target reduction on the amount of GHG emissions from a baseline year (which is 1990 in the context of the UK's carbon targets). The Climate Change Act 2008 originally set a target of an 80% reduction in GHG emissions by 2050.

A carbon budget places a legally binding restriction on the total amount of GHGs that the UK can emit over a certain five-year period. GHGs include CO2 but also six other GHGs (such as methane and nitrous oxide) that are harmful to the environment in line with the Kyoto Protocol.

Under the Climate Change Act 2008, the government must set a carbon budget 12 years in advance covering the years 2008–2050. The first three carbon budgets (Carbon Budgets 1, 2 and 3) covering the years 2008–2022 were set under the Carbon Budgets Order 2009[12] and the most recent carbon budget (Carbon Budget 6) was set in 2021 at 965 million tonnes of CO2 equivalent for the period 2033–2037.[13]

In 2019, following advice from the CCC, the government committed to reaching net zero emissions by 2050, which is of course a 100% GHG emissions reduction target from 1990. This was enacted into UK law by the Climate Change Act 2008 (2050 Target Amendment) Order 2019.[14] This aligns with the general consensus under the 2015 Paris Agreement that, in order to keep global warming below 1.5°C above pre-industrial levels, global GHG emissions need to reach net zero by 2050. To reach this target, the government has committed to ensure all UK transport will be net zero by 2050.[15]

How the government sets out to achieve this is down to the particular government at any given moment, and this is why we thought it important to address the state of political uncertainty within the UK at the date of publication. While the government (whoever that may be and from whichever party they may be from) has, to date, always accepted the advice of the CCC on carbon budgets and carbon targets themselves, it has not always adopted ideas proposed by the CCC on how to meet those targets. For example, in September 2023, the

The UK was the first major economy to set legally binding carbon targets, enforced by setting carbon budgets, over 15 years ago.

then-Prime Minister Rishi Sunak announced that the target for ending the sale of non-zero emission cars and vans would be put back five years from 2030 to 2035, a move which, in the CCC's view would dent consumer confidence.[16] It is understood from its manifesto that the current Labour government intends to reintroduce the 2030 deadline but this has yet to be formalised into law at the time of writing.

However, since 2008 and with increasing frequency as climate change takes precedence on local, national and global agendas, there have been a number of reports, proposals and subsequent announcements from the government to put into place plans to allay climate change and meet these carbon targets. What we consider to be the most important of those in respect of transport are set out in the following sections. This is intended to be an overview of the government's approach to decarbonisation in the transport sector and the level of importance that the government places on this sector.

7. Transport and meeting the UK's climate targets

In 2008, the CCC's first report, "Building a low-carbon economy – the UK's contribution to tackling climate change" (the '2008 Report'), recognised that reducing domestic transport emissions was one of four key ways for the UK to meet the first three carbon budgets.[17]

The 2008 Report found that domestic transport emissions had increased by 9% between 1990 and 2006 and accounted for around 24% of all CO2 emissions from the UK's national inventory. This was the second highest proportion of emissions, only behind emissions associated with industry, such as factories and manufacturing.

It recognised that in respect of domestic transport emissions, "[s]ignificant potential for emissions reductions exists through changed driver behaviour, modal shift and better journey planning"[18] and, as we will see throughout this Special Report, this is essentially still the case over 15 years later.

'Modal shift' refers to encouraging a transition from high emission modes of transport, such as private cars, to low emission alternatives like public transit, cycling and walking. The UK has been promoting modal shift through investment in public transport infrastructure, cycling lanes and pedestrian-friendly urban planning. Moreover, the government has been advocating for flexible working arrangements and telecommuting to reduce overall travel demand.

Between 1990 and 2006, private road transport (cars, vans and HGVs) accounted for 86% of total transport emissions in the UK, with 4% from buses, 2% from rail and 2% from domestic aviation.[19] The focus of the 2008 Report, and indeed future government reports on transport

The UK has been promoting modal shift through investment in public transport infrastructure, cycling lanes and pedestrian-friendly urban planning. Moreover, the government has been advocating for flexible working arrangements and telecommuting to reduce overall travel demand.

in the UK, was therefore on abatement opportunities in private road vehicles.

In this respect, the 2008 Report described the potential of two (at the time) relatively new vehicle technologies – electric vehicles (EVs) and hydrogen. These are explored in detail in Chapter III.

Subsequent reports from both the CCC and others follow a similar approach to decarbonising transport and the important role it will play if the UK is to reach its climate targets. We discuss the main reports below.

8. Road to Zero Strategy

In September 2018, the UK's Department for Transport (DfT) published the Road to Zero Strategy as part of the government's Industrial Strategy and zoned in on cleaner road transport and the design and manufacturing of ZEVs.[20] It set out key policies in relation to:

- reducing emissions from vehicles already on the roads – through low carbon fuels and measures to encourage fuel-efficient motoring; and
- driving uptake of cleaner new vehicles – through vehicle

emission regulations, grants for plug-in cars and setting up a Road Transport Emissions Advice Group.

The most significant impact was to ban the sale of new petrol and diesel cars and vans by 2040. As will be seen throughout this section, this specific deadline has since been subject to change on multiple occasions. Successive governments have pushed this forward to 2030 (in "Decarbonising Transport: A Better, Greener Britain" published in July 2021) then backwards to 2035 (as announced by then-Prime Minister Rishi Sunak in September 2023). This will likely be brought forward again to 2030 if the Labour government's 2024 election pledge is implemented.

This is one example of the ever-shifting political landscape upon which a government makes policies and it highlights the importance of keeping up to date on major policy developments that will impact the transport industry.

9. The UK's Ten Point Plan for a Green Industrial Revolution[21]

In November 2020, amid the COVID-19 pandemic, the government launched the "Ten Point Plan for a Green Industrial Revolution" setting out the government's priorities on achieving net zero by 2050. Three of the 10 points involve transport:

- accelerating the shift to ZEVs;
- green public transport, cycling and walking; and
- jet zero and green ships.

While covered in this section below, each of these areas are also covered in more detail in other chapters of this Special Report.

9.1 Zero emission vehicles

The Ten Point Plan recognised that ZEVs could be the "most visible incarnation of [the] ability to simultaneously create jobs, strengthen British industry, cut emissions and continue travelling".[22] It set out a package of investments including up to £1 billion to support the electrification of vehicles and their supply chains and £1.3 billion to accelerate the roll out of charging infrastructure, with an expectation for there to be more than 2,500 high-powered charge points on motorways and major A roads by 2030, rising to around 6,000 by 2035.

The Ten Point Plan also declared the government's commitment to ban the sale of new petrol and diesel cars and vans by 2030 (bringing it forward from the 2040 deadline first introduced by the Road to Zero Strategy). This commitment was delayed to 2035 following the announcement on 20 September 2023 by then-Prime Minister Rishi

Sunak. It is understood the 2030 deadline will be reinstated by the new Labour government following the 2024 election.

There were also a number of milestones set out for 2021, including for the government to publish a delivery plan setting out key milestones for the phase out of petrol and diesel cars, a consultation on the phase out of new diesel HGVs and a Green Paper on the UK's post-EU emissions regulations. These were consulted on in 2021/22 and resulted in the Zero Emission Vehicle Mandate, discussed in more detail Chapter III.

9.2 Green public transport, cycling and walking

This section of the Ten Point Plan recognises the importance of modal shift from private car usage to more sustainable options like public transport, cycling and walking – particularly in urban areas – to reduce congestion and emissions. This is a common theme throughout much of the government's approach. Although the Ten Point Plan focused on the level of investments to be put into public transport, this does not happen in a vacuum – it needs to happen alongside a campaign to get the public using the infrastructure being invested in.

The Ten Point Plan followed an announcement in February 2020 that the government pledged to invest £4.2 billion in city public transport

Although the Ten Point Plan focused on the level of investments to be put into public transport, this does not happen in a vacuum – it needs to happen alongside a campaign to get the public using the infrastructure being invested in.

and £5 billion on buses. Several key milestones focused on bus transport, including by early 2021 for the government to publish its national bus strategy "Bus Back Better" and the first new zero emission buses to be delivered.

Buses are an important part of the government's decarbonisation strategy because if more people use the bus, fewer people use private cars. It is also easier to control the amount of buses that are lower emissions or electrified – it would involve a change in operator policy or investment which can be encouraged by the government through subsidies and preferential taxation. Private car use is more piecemeal and involves car owners selling their current car and replacing it – something that is expensive and arduous – meaning it is more difficult for the government to implement. The importance of a modal shift to increased use of public transport is covered in more detail in Chapter IV.

In accordance with the Ten Point Plan, the DfT published "Bus Back Better" in March 2021,[23] the first strategy of its kind in the UK. The government recognised that rail, road, aviation, cycling and walking all had previously been covered, and that buses had never had long-term funding commitments. It highlighted several issues with the current bus systems, including poor integration between operators, complex ticketing and lack of evening services. It set out a plan for buses outside of London, using the London bus system as a quasi-role model for how the government envisages buses to run in other cities.

Buses have been an immediate focus of the new Labour government with Labour's manifesto pledging to "reform the broken system" and "give local communities in England control over routes and schedules".[24] The new Secretary of State for Transport, Louise Haigh, spent her first official visit in Manchester where she pledged to "support local leaders to deliver better buses".[25] The Bee Network in Manchester is the first bus franchise in England outside of London and it is anticipated that similar schemes will be rolled out across the UK in due course.

The Ten Point Plan also briefly touched on plans to expand rail routes in 'big regional cities' and electrify regional and other rail routes.

Beyond buses and rail, the Ten Point Plan also highlighted the importance of increased walking and cycling as forms of transport. It announced investments in 'active transport schemes' such as cycle lanes, as well as low traffic neighbourhoods. It set out plans to encourage more people to cycle through cycling training in every school by 2025. Similar initiatives are observable across various European countries, with cities like Copenhagen (Denmark) and

Amsterdam (Netherlands) implementing innovative policies to prioritise cycling and public transport over private car use.

9.3 Jet zero and green ships

The third section of the Ten Point Plan to deal with transport covers the government's plan to drive the uptake of sustainable aviation fuel, investments in developing zero emission aircraft and developing infrastructure at airports and seaports.

The Ten Point Plan established the Jet Zero Council as a sector-wide partnership to accelerate the development and adoption of new technologies to help develop the government's strategy to reach net zero aviation. Further investments into developing zero emission aircraft and clean maritime technology were also announced, highlighting the fact that there were already hydrogen ferry trials at Orkney and plans to launch a hydrogen refuelling port in Teesside.

Another key theme was around the investment into sustainable aviation fuel (SAF) and consultations on SAF mandates to blend greener fuels into jet fuel used in aircraft to immediately reduce emissions. The new Labour government will introduce a new revenue support mechanism for domestic SAF production and an SAF mandate,[26] and it is anticipated that aviation will be a key area of development over the coming years. SAF and other sustainable aviation technologies are covered in Chapter VII.

10. The UK's transport decarbonisation plan

In July 2021, the government published its transport decarbonisation plan, "Decarbonising Transport: A Better, Greener Britain" ('the TDP'). This could be said to be the key proposal specific to the decarbonisation of transport that we have seen from the government to date. It was last updated (at the time of writing) in January 2023.[27]

The TDP included declarations by the government around the following key topics:

- *Increasing active travel:* The government pledged to invest £2 billion over five years to encourage 50% of journeys in towns and cities to be by cycling or walking.
- *Zero emission buses and coaches:* The government pledged to deliver the national bus strategy (see above) and aimed to support the introduction of 4,000 new zero emission buses and the enabling infrastructure. The TDP also noted that there would be consultation on the phase out of the sale of new non-zero emission buses and coaches.
- *Decarbonising the railways:* The government pledged a net zero railway by 2050. The action plan for this includes removing all

The Hydrogen Strategy considered early on how hydrogen can be used in the transport industry. It focuses on bolstering domestic hydrogen production and utilisation in heavy duty transport, maritime vessels and public transit systems.

diesel-only trains (passenger and freight) from the network by 2040 and increasing electrification as well as supporting the development of battery and hydrogen trains. Other initiatives include growing capacity to enable a greater modal shift from road and air and modernising ticketing for easier travel.

- *Zero emission cars, vans and bikes/scooters:* The main pledge here was to phase out combustion engine vehicles by 2030. In terms of the government's own car fleet, there is a pledge for that to be zero emission by 2027.
- *Maritime decarbonisation:* The TDP set out net zero ambitions for the UK domestic maritime sector, with indicative targets from 2030. The government pledged to have a consultation on the ban on combustion engine in domestic vessels and a pledge to extend the Renewable Transport Fuel Obligation to shipping.
- *Aviation decarbonisation:* The government confirmed there would be a consultation on the UK 'Jet Zero' strategy and a further consultation on setting a target for UK domestic aviation to reach net zero by 2040. The TDP set out pledges to support the development of zero carbon aircraft and zero emission flight infrastructure at UK airports, and to encourage the commercialisation of SAFs.

The key enablers the government identified included:

- the role of hydrogen;
- the role of sustainable low carbon fuels; and
- modal shift and better use of road vehicles (higher occupancy and car sharing).

We have addressed each of these areas in this Special Report (albeit we have grouped them slightly differently to reflect our views on how each of the modes of transport and the enablers will work together to decarbonise the transport sector to support the UK's net zero ambitions).

The CCC responded to the TDP in July 2021[28] and noted that the overall ambition of the TDP aligns with the CCC recommendations.

The 'devil will be in the detail' and the CCC said it looked forward to scrutinising the government's proposals while awaiting "delivery of other key roadmaps on heating, hydrogen, food, biomass, the Treasury's Net Zero Review, and the Government's overall Net Zero Strategy".[29] We cover the Net Zero Strategy in section 12 below.

11. UK Hydrogen Strategy

The UK Hydrogen Strategy was published in August 2021.[30] The Hydrogen Strategy recognised the importance of low carbon hydrogen by stating that "[h]ydrogen is likely to be fundamental to achieving net zero in transport" and that "it is also likely to provide solutions for sectors that will not be able to fully decarbonise otherwise, including aviation and shipping".

The Hydrogen Strategy considered early on how hydrogen can be used in the transport industry. It focuses on bolstering domestic hydrogen production and utilisation in heavy duty transport, maritime vessels and public transit systems. It also encourages international collaboration in research and development.

12. Net Zero Strategy: Build Back Greener[31] and Powering Up Britain: Net Zero Growth Plan[32]

The government announced its Net Zero Strategy in October 2021 ('Net Zero Strategy 2021') which set out a series of policies and commitments designed to enable the UK to reach net zero by 2050.

It included measures to deliver emissions reductions to meet targets up to the sixth carbon budget (which covers the period between 2033 and 2037).

The Net Zero Growth Plan, published on 30 March 2023, set out more detail on how the UK government aims to reach net zero by 2050. This followed a successful legal challenge to the 2021 Net Zero Strategy, where the High Court ruled that it did not set out enough detail on how the proposed policies would meet the carbon budgets.

The Net Zero Strategy 2021 (as updated) sets out the proposals and policies for decarbonising all sectors of the UK economy, including transport.

13. Electric vehicle infrastructure strategy[33]

"Taking charge: the electric vehicle infrastructure strategy" (the 'EV Strategy') was published by the government in March 2022. The EV strategy highlighted the fact that in December 2021, over 25% of all new cars sold in the UK were battery-powered EVs. In 2019, this figure was just 2%. This shows a rapid increase in the number of EVs being sold in comparison to traditional petrol or diesel vehicles and highlights the importance of the UK's infrastructure being able to keep up with this.

By 2030, the government said in the EV Strategy that it expects there to be around 300,000 public charge points as a minimum in the UK, but there could potentially be more than double that number. Public charge points are necessary for long distance journeys and for those households that do not have private driveways to enable them to charge their vehicles overnight.

14. Carbon Budget Delivery Plan and ZEV Mandate

In March 2023, the UK government launched the Carbon Budget Delivery Plan, which recognises that the switch to EVs is the largest single driver of future emissions reduction in the UK's Net Zero pathway. Switching to EVs is expected to account for approximately one-fifth (50 MtCO2e/year) of the annual savings on carbon emissions by 2035.[34]

On 28 September 2023, the Conservative government also confirmed a ZEV mandate would apply from January 2024. The ZEV mandate will require 80% of new cars and 70% of new vans sold in the UK to be zero emission by 2030, increasing to 100% by 2035. This has been implemented into law by the Vehicle Emissions Trading Scheme Order 2023.[35]

15. The UK general election 2024

On 4 July 2024, the UK held a general election which resulted in a change of government from the Conservative party to the Labour party.

Newly appointed Secretary of State for Transport, Louise Haigh, set out her five strategic priorities for the transport sector on 8 July 2024.[36] These are:

- improving performance on the railways and driving forward rail reform;
- improving bus services and growing usage across the country;
- transforming infrastructure to work for the whole country, promoting social mobility and tackling regional inequality;
- delivering greener transport; and
- better integrating transport networks.

The Labour manifesto also set out a number of pledges relating to transport, including an overhaul of Britain's railways, the creation of Great British Railways and new powers for local leaders to franchise local bus services.[37] It is clear that these, along with the five strategic priorities set out above, will impact the policies and approaches described in this chapter that have been created by previous governments.

At the time of writing, there has been a flurry of reports, data and bills published across the UK government website and across many industries but these are all early-stage initiatives and are not yet formalised into action plans or consultations. We should expect a number of formal policy papers and consultations to follow in due course. It will be necessary over the coming months and years to closely monitor these developments as they crystalise into policies, regulations and law.

16. Middle East approach to decarbonisation

The most recent COP, COP28, was held in November/December 2023 in Dubai. The choice of location was met with some criticism as Dubai, and the Middle East in general, has traditionally been known for its vast oil reserves and high carbon emissions. Despite the region's heavy reliance on fossil fuels, there is a growing recognition in the region of the need to transition towards a more sustainable, low-carbon future.

The Middle East has seen regional cooperation towards decarbonisation. The Middle East Green Initiative (MGI) is a regional effort led by Saudi Arabia to mitigate the impact of climate change on the region and to collaborate to meet global climate targets. The current MGI targets are to reduce 670 million tonnes of CO2 emissions across the region and plant 50 billion trees across the Middle East. A number of initiatives of the MGI include the establishment of a regional centre for carbon extraction, use and storage and the implementation of a circular carbon economy.

In respect of transport, Dubai has been promoting the use of EVs to reduce emissions and the Dubai Electricity and Water Authority has installed numerous EV charging stations across the city. The Dubai government also offers incentives such as free public parking and exemptions from tolls and registration fees for EV owners. Saudi Arabia has also implemented fuel economy standards for light-duty vehicles, aiming to reduce fuel consumption and CO2 emissions. It is worth noting that several European countries, including Norway, the Netherlands and Sweden, have already made remarkable strides in EV adoption. Norway, in particular, stands out as a global leader in EV market share, attributing its success to a combination of generous incentives, reduced taxes and extensive charging infrastructure.

To encourage a modal shift from private car travel which is prevalent in Dubai, the Roads and Transport Authority in Dubai is modernising its public transport and the Dubai Autonomous Transportation Strategy aims to transform 25% of total public transportation in Dubai to autonomous mode by 2030.

Saudi Arabia's National Strategy for Transport and Logistics aims to reduce carbon emissions of transport by 25% by 2030. To do so, the Transport General Authority issued a trial operating licence for hydrogen train technology in late 2023[38] and signed a deal for a large intercity bus transport project.[39]

Comparatively, other European countries, such as Germany and Norway, have also demonstrated a strong commitment to hydrogen. Germany, for instance, is actively promoting hydrogen-powered trains and buses. Norway is implementing hydrogen-based ferries and maritime vessels. While each country's approach varies, the underlying intent is to harness hydrogen's potential as a clean energy source.

The Middle East has substantial solar energy potential, and many countries are capitalising on this. The UAE has set a target to generate 50% of its energy from clean sources by 2050 and as part of the Dubai Clean Energy Strategy, the Mohammed bin Rashid Al Maktoum Solar Park is set to be the largest single-site solar park in the world based on the 'independent power producer' model. It will have a capacity of 5,000 megawatts by 2030.

Saudi Arabia, the world's largest oil exporter, has also launched the ambitious Vision 2030 programme, which includes a significant focus on renewable energy. The country aims to produce 50% of its electricity from renewables by 2030.

While the Middle East continues to face significant challenges in decarbonising its economy, there is a clear and growing commitment to this transition. The region's abundant solar potential, combined with efforts in carbon capture and decarbonising the transport sector provides a solid foundation for a sustainable, low-carbon future. The Middle East's efforts in decarbonising the transport sector are diverse and significant, ranging from promoting electric and hydrogen vehicles, improving public transport and implementing fuel economy standards. These initiatives are crucial steps towards reducing the region's carbon footprint and achieving a sustainable future.

17. Conclusion

International collaboration will be important in the race to net zero, particularly in sectors like aviation and shipping that transcend national boundaries. Nations are implementing decarbonisation strategies at different paces and with different focuses. This is only natural when you consider the different stages of development and the different challenges that are faced by, for example, the UK compared with Saudi Arabia. The common theme, however, is a recognition that the transport sector is a large contributor to GHG emissions and the implementation of greener transport options will be fundamental to global efforts to reach net zero targets by 2050. The rest of this Special Report delves further into the different modes of transport and the efforts being made in each of these towards achieving a more sustainable future for the global transport sector.

Notes

1 Hannah Ritchie, "Cars, planes, trains: where do CO2 emissions from transport come from?", Our World in Data, 6 October 2020, https://ourworldindata.org/co2-emissions-from-transport#:~:text=The%20IEA%20looks%20at%20CO,Perspectives%202020%2C%20IEA%2C%20Paris.
2 Intergovernmental Panel on Climate Change (IPCC), "Climate Change: The IPCC 1990 and 1992 Assessments", June 1992, www.ipcc.ch/report/climate-change-the-ipcc-1990-and-1992-assessments/.
3 Kyoto Protocol to the UNFCC, 11 December 1997, https://assets.publishing.service.gov.uk/media/5a7c810140f0b626628ac866/5379.pdf.
4 UN, "Paris Agreement – Status of Ratification", https://unfccc.int/process/the-paris-agreement/status-of-ratification.
5 Department of Energy and Climate Change, "UK Climate Change Programme", 2006, https://webarchive.nationalarchives.gov.uk/ukgwa/20110405153917/http://www.decc.gov.uk/en/content/cms/what_we_do/change_energy/tackling_clima/programme/programme.aspx.
6 Section 33 of the Climate Change Act 2008.
7 *Ibid*, Section 34.
8 *Ibid*, Section 38.
9 *Ibid*, Section 36.
10 See www.theccc.org.uk/publicationtype/0-report/02-progress-reports/.
11 UK Government press release, "Chris Stark to lead Mission Control to deliver clean power by 2030", 9 July 2004, www.gov.uk/government/news/chris-stark-to-lead-mission-control-to-deliver-clean-power-by-2030.
12 Carbon Budgets Order 2009 (SI 2009 No 1259).
13 Carbon Budget Order 2021 (SI 2021 No 750).
14 SI 2019 No 1056.
15 Department for Transport (DfT), "Decarbonising Transport: A Better, Greener Britain", 2021, https://assets.publishing.service.gov.uk/government/uploads/system/uploads/attachment_data/file/1009448/decarbonising-transport-a-better-greener-britain.pdf.

16 Climate Change Committee (CCC), "CCC assessment of recent announcements and developments on Net Zero", 12 October 2023, www.theccc.org.uk/2023/10/12/ccc-assessment-of-recent-announcements-and-developments-on-net-zero/.
17 CCC, Part II, Section 7 of the 2008 Report: "Setting and meeting the first three budgets – Reducing domestic transport emissions", www.theccc.org.uk/publication/building-a-low-carbon-economy-the-uks-contribution-to-tackling-climate-change-2/.
18 CCC, 2008 Report, "Executive summary", p27.
19 *Ibid*, p284.
20 DfT, "The Road to Zero", 2018, https://assets.publishing.service.gov.uk/media/5b968e3ee5274a13859deed2/road-to-zero.pdf.
21 HM Government, "The Ten Point Plan for a Green Industrial Revolution", November 2020, https://assets.publishing.service.gov.uk/media/5fb5513de90e0720978b1a6f/10_POINT_PLAN_BOOKLET.pdf.
22 *Ibid*, p14.
23 DfT, "Bus Back Better", 2021, https://assets.publishing.service.gov.uk/media/6086912fd3bf7f013c8f4510/DfT-Bus-Back-Better-national-bus-strategy-for-England.pdf.
24 See https://labour.org.uk/change/kickstart-economic-growth/#transport.
25 UK Government press release, "Transport Secretary kickstarts 'bus solution' as she promises to support local leaders t deliver better buses up and down the country", 11 July 2024, www.gov.uk/government/news/transport-secretary-kickstarts-bus-revolution-as-she-promises-to-support-local-leaders-to-deliver-better-buses-up-and-down-the-country.
26 See n 15 above.
27 Sustainable Aviation Fuel (Revenue Support Mechanism Bill), www.gov.uk/government/speeches/sustainable-aviation-fuel-initiatives.
28 CCC, "CCC responds to Government's Transport Decarbonisation Plan", 14 July 2021, www.theccc.org.uk/2021/07/14/ccc-responds-to-governments-transport-decarbonisation-plan/.
29 *Ibid.*
30 HM Government, "UK Hydrogen Strategy", (CP 475), August 2021, https://assets.publishing.service.gov.uk/government/uploads/system/uploads/attachment_data/file/1175494/UK-Hydrogen-Strategy_web.pdf.
31 HM Government, "Net Zero Strategy: Build Back Greener", October 2021, https://assets.publishing.service.gov.uk/media/6194dfa4d3bf7f0555071b1b/net-zero-strategy-beis.pdf.
32 HM Government, Policy Paper, "Powering Up Britain: Net Zero Growth Plan", updated 4 April 2024, www.gov.uk/government/publications/powering-up-britain/powering-up-britain-net-zero-growth- plan.
33 DfT, Policy Paper, "UK electric vehicle infrastructure strategy", March 2022, www.gov.uk/government/publications/uk-electric-vehicle-infrastructure-strategy.
34 CCC, "Letter: Zero-emission vehicle mandate", 28 September 2023, www.theccc.org.uk/publication/letter-zero-emission-vehicle-mandate/.
35 Vehicle Emissions Trading Schemes Order 2023 (SI 2023 No 1394).
36 See www.gov.uk/government/news/transport-secretary-sets-out-5-key-priorities-to-deliver-the-biggest-overhaul-to-transport-in-a-generation.
37 See https://labour.org.uk/change/kickstart-economic-growth/#transport.
38 World Economic Forum, "Autonomous mobility: 3 lessons for success from Saudi Arabia", 16 October 2023, www.weforum.org/agenda/2023/10/saudi-arabia-s-roadmap-to-autonomous- mobility-3-key-aspects-for-success/.
39 The largest project for transporting passengers by buses connecting the Saudi cities, through a transportation network that covers more than 200 cities and governorates.

II. Rail decarbonisation

Martin Fleetwood
Ross Sandford
Rachel Scott
Addleshaw Goddard

1. The legal imperative: United Kingdom

1.1 Role of rail decarbonisation in meeting legal commitments

Under the Climate Change Act 2008, the UK government has a legally binding commitment to reduce greenhouse gas (GHG) emissions by 100% from 1990 levels (the so-called 'net zero' target by 2050). Compared to other modes of transport, such as road and aviation, rail is a low contributor to GHG emissions in the transport sector. In the UK, figures from the Rail Safety and Standards Board issued in 2023 show that rail contributed only 1.4% of domestic transport GHG emissions and roughly 0.5% of the UK's total GHG emissions.[1]

Nonetheless, many trains rely on diesel fuel to provide propulsion (known as 'traction power'), so moving away from the use of diesel fuel to alternative forms of traction power has a role to play in meeting net zero and there are various policy commitments reflecting this. Further, there is a clearer path to reducing emissions caused by rail travel than there is for alternative forms of travel, such as aviation. As more work is undertaken to reduce rail emissions, it will strengthen arguments to encourage modal shift from road and aviation to rail. For example, carbon emissions for rail freight are "around a quarter of the CO2 equivalent emissions of HGVs, per tonne mile travelled".[2]

1.2 UK government policy

In the UK, the Department for Transport (DfT) published the Rail Environment Policy Statement in July 2021[3] setting out a direction for the rail industry on environmental sustainability and outlining policy priorities on matters including traction decarbonisation and decarbonisation of the rail estate. Alongside this, it also published its Decarbonising Transport[4] plan, which made specific policy commitments in relation to rail decarbonisation, including commitments to encourage greater modal shift of passengers and freight from road to rail, incentivise the early take up of low carbon traction for rail freight and indicated an ambition to "take all diesel-only trains off the track" in England and Wales by 2040.[5]

The Scottish government has made similar commitments to modal shift and traction decarbonisation in its Rail Services Decarbonisation Action Plan,[6] although it is more ambitious in relation to the removal of diesel-only trains, with these set to be phased out in Scotland by 2035.

1.3 UK rail industry strategy

Network Rail (which owns and maintains most of the UK's railway network) published a Traction Decarbonisation Network Strategy[7]

It is recognised that improved rail integration (as part of a sustainable transport network for both goods and passengers) is required to enable modal shift. This will be facilitated through the creation of a cross-sector working group focused on integrated transport.

in 2020 which set out recommendations about how to achieve decarbonisation. This envisaged a rolling programme of electrification of 13,000 single track kilometres. However, a subsequent 2021 Government Spending Review publication determined this to be unaffordable, so alternatives will need to be considered.

(a) Sustainable Rail Blueprint (SRB)
An industry-wide sustainability strategy for rail in the UK is being facilitated by the Rail Safety and Standards Board (RSSB) with oversight from the DfT. The Sustainable Rail Blueprint (SRB) was published in November 2023 following consultation with the rail industry in May 2022.[8] The SRB identifies six common solutions, which set out "how the rail industry can successfully deliver against its sustainability objectives". These common solutions[9] are as follows:

"Zero Emission Traction" – there must be a clear investment pathway to clean, decarbonised traction: The Great British Railways Transition Team (GBRTT) is a body established by the DfT to enable strategic reform of the rail sector, particularly the provision of railway infrastructure in the UK and government-let public service contracts for passenger services in England. GBRTT is tasked with providing a detailed strategy for the delivery of modern, green train services within its long-term strategy for rail. This includes targeted electrification of lines and maximising the value of alternative rolling stock solutions as well as considering other solutions, including bi-modes, battery, hydrogen and sustainable fuels.

"Seamless Journeys" – rail must fully integrate as part of a sustainable, joined-up transport system to support the shift of people and goods onto railways: It is recognised that improved rail integration (as part of a sustainable transport network for both goods and passengers) is required to enable modal shift. This will be facilitated through the creation of a cross-sector working group focused on integrated transport.

"Nature-based Solutions" – an industry-wide approach to nature-based solutions is needed, to maximise the social and environmental benefits of rail industry land: This solution would make use of the 60,000 hectares of land and natural capital that is owned and managed by the railways, utilising the Network Rail Sustainable Land Use Strategic Framework to implement nature-based solutions including lineside vegetation, natural habitats and other green infrastructure (including green roofs and living walls which will deliver enhanced biodiversity and contribute to net zero while reducing flood risk).

"Social Value" – social value must be adopted and embedded across the industry to increase quality of life and maximise the benefits of rail to society: The rail industry is tasked with utilising the Rail Social Value Tool[10] to adopt and embed a consistent approach to social value.

"Data Framework" – a data framework is needed to measure, collate and report progress against sustainable rail goals: Establishing a data framework will allow for analysis of performance and progress against a common set of performance metrics, which will provide for benchmarking and will enable targeted action while guiding investment decisions.

"Culture for Sustainability" – making sustainability part of everything we do must be a core pillar of the culture of the rail industry: Environmental and social sustainability must be embedded into business decisions so that opportunities are considered at all stages of a project.

(b) Strategic Programme Business Case

Alongside the SRB, GBRTT is working with the government to develop a Strategic Programme Business Case (SPBC) which will model different scenarios to a net zero network by 2050. The SPBC will be utilised to help determine the best options for delivery, taking into account affordability and deliverability and will identify priority schemes where benefits can be most efficiently implemented.

The solutions currently being proposed take a clear net zero position rather than a complete removal of diesel fuel from the power supply system. As noted above, the industry solutions need to prioritise those schemes which make the most progress towards net zero and for some freight-only routes with significant power requirements for the trains, diesel fuel (or similar) remains the most effective option in 2050. However, with the continuing development of technology across all transport sectors, it is possible that a viable alternative will have become available by then.

1.4 Other rail industry strategies outside the UK

Rail decarbonisation strategies vary across different countries, but are not dissimilar to those of the UK, with focus often being on the following:

(a) Electrification

Many countries have focused on electrifying their rail networks over a number of years to reduce carbon emissions. This generally involves replacing diesel-powered trains with electric trains that draw power from overhead wires. In addition, most new lines are built with overhead wires as the primary power source.[11]

Many countries have focused on electrifying their rail networks over a number of years to reduce carbon emissions. This generally involves replacing diesel-powered trains with electric trains that draw power from overhead wires. In addition, most new lines are built with overhead wires as the primary power source.

(b) Hydrogen-powered trains

Hydrogen-powered trains are being explored as an alternative to diesel trains. These trains use fuel cells that convert hydrogen into electricity to power the train. Germany and France have been market leaders in testing and implementing hydrogen trains.

(c) Battery-powered trains

Battery technology is being used to power trains without the need for electrified infrastructure. Battery-powered trains can be recharged at stations or through regenerative braking. Countries such as Japan and the Netherlands have been experimenting with battery-powered trains as low-cost alternatives to electrification.

(d) Biofuels

In the United States, there are currently a number of trials being conducted to assess the viability of different types of biofuels, either created from biomass or recycling biodegradable waste outputs. Biofuel trials are also being undertaken in Brazil, Southeast Asia, Australia and India. A common factor is the need to have power sources which can take a train over very long distances where there may be limited frequency of services and potentially challenging weather conditions. In such cases, it is very difficult to justify investment in overhead electrification and refuelling/recharging points are few and far between.

(e) Renewable energy procurement

Some countries are focusing on sourcing renewable energy to power their rail networks. This involves purchasing electricity generated from renewable sources like wind, solar, or hydroelectric power. Switzerland, for example, has committed to using 100% renewable energy for its rail network. However, this does require a relatively comprehensive overhead electricity network to be most effective.

(f) Modal shift and improved efficiency

Encouraging a shift from road and air travel to rail can help reduce overall carbon emissions. Improving rail efficiency through route optimisation, reducing energy consumption and implementing smart systems can also contribute to decarbonisation efforts. Many countries, including Japan and Sweden, have implemented measures to promote modal shift and improve the efficiency of journeys by rail, both for passengers and freight.

Many of these topics will be addressed further in respect of the UK later in this chapter.

Encouraging a shift from road and air travel to rail can help reduce overall carbon emissions. Improving rail efficiency through route optimisation, reducing energy consumption and implementing smart systems can also contribute to decarbonisation efforts.

2. Technology: "What does the future look like?"

2.1 Managing a two-part solution

Within the road, maritime and aviation sectors, the power solutions being proposed are primarily based on the vehicles, vessels and airframes themselves having self-contained power systems (eg, batteries for cars and alternative aviation fuels for aircraft). Refuelling or recharging facilities are provided at specific locations, but the 'go anywhere' nature of their use means that generally the infrastructure which those vehicles, vessels and airframes use or travel on remains more or less unaffected by the changes in drive technology.

The rail sector on the other hand is very much restricted to the sets of rails on which its trains run and the availability of power supplies (particularly for those routes which have been electrified). This has the effect of imposing significant changes to the railway infrastructure as alternatives to diesel fuel are implemented. Consequently, the effects of making the change to net zero need to consider the potentially significant financial costs of infrastructure upgrades as well as the carbon cost of these works.

While most passenger services only operate within a region or on a certain route type within the overall route network, allowing a specific replacement power solution to be developed for them, the position for freight services is less easy. The freight sector operates a number of services where there is the likelihood that its trains will need access to different parts of a country's railway infrastructure which are primarily designed for a particular power source. This means that such trains will most likely require the ability to work using more than one type of power source. However, including multiple power sources in one locomotive can bring technological challenges – limiting the number of options available – as well as increasing the cost of these locomotives, both in terms of initial purchase price and the lifetime maintenance costs.

The effectiveness of a power source is not just a factor of the raw power at the driver's disposal. Other external factors can play their part and need to be evaluated and controlled. This is especially true once you look at alternatives to full electrification such as batteries.[12] Detailed analysis of the aerodynamics of the train can lead to a change in the body shape which reduces wind resistance while different bogie components can reduce the resistance between the wheels and rails. Using an intelligent energy management system which understands the route characteristics and stopping patterns can make best use of gradients, speed limits and train weights to reduce the draw on the power supply. Use of regenerative breaking will also help to recover energy when the train is using its brakes.

What may appear to be the optimum solution for providing the necessary power requirements may not be cost effective or particularly suitable for any given location.

In deciding which power solution is suitable for the rail industry there are, therefore, a number of factors which need to be taken into account. What may appear to be the optimum solution for providing the necessary power requirements may not be cost effective or particularly suitable for any given location. This, in turn, creates additional issues for the train operators particularly given that the charges for accessing infrastructure is a significant cost for them. Persuading industry to manage these costs when implementing net zero solutions and sharing them equitably between industry parties is a factor which should not be ignored in rail's net zero journey.

2.2 Electrification

Considering the carbon that is produced in generating electricity, an electric train still emits significantly less carbon per mile than a diesel train. As more electricity is generated using renewable sources this will only decrease further. Electrification of the railway network is therefore a key way to decarbonise rail transport.

There are two main types of traction electrification system in the UK: (i) overhead lines (OLE) which carry the power to the trains through lines suspended above the rail network; and (ii) third rail, in which the power is provided via a conductor rail next to the running rail.

This technology is not new, with versions having been around for over 100 years, and is already widely used. Around 42% of the rail network in the UK is already electrified, while in several other European countries the proportion is significantly higher at 50–60% of all rail lines.

Given that OLE systems can provide more power to the train than through a third rail sited alongside the running lines, there is limited research into power collection systems for third rail systems. The drive system within the train is essentially the same except for managing the fact that the power supplied is direct current rather than alternating current. Manufacturers are generally able to provide either an OLE version or third rail version of the same train, so where OLE is available, this is likely to provide the electricity system of choice in the future.

For lines where trains travel at over 100 mph or the route is part of the core freight network, electrification is (currently) the only realistic option. Many manufacturers make electric trains, and the technology is not expected to have changed significantly by 2050. The main difference is likely to be an ability to manage discontinuous electrification – short gaps in the OLE where it is difficult to install due to cost and existing structures. Trains will be able to hold an amount of energy to allow them to travel over these gaps without a perceived loss of power.

The railway's infrastructure and the location of the system will continue to provide barriers to fully electrifying existing rail networks. A key issue is the significant engineering work required as well as its cost. Support for the overhead wires needs to be sufficiently robust to deal with the relevant climate (including anticipated effects of climate change), a number of existing bridges will need to be replaced and existing tunnels enlarged to fit in the necessary clearance between the train and the overhead wire and also between the overhead wire and various lineside structures. This means there can be very substantial cost, time and disruption involved in installing OLE, particularly on heavily engineered sections of track.

The high cost of installing OLE (whatever its specification) is expected to mean that it will not be cost effective to install such systems to enable full electrification of an entire rail system and alternatives for those other parts will be needed. In addition to trains just using externally provided electricity there will be a need for trains which contain a secondary power source (bi-modes) to reach the outer limits of the rail network.

The future railway of 2050 is likely to see all main passenger routes using OLE for at least most of those routes (with some discontinuous electrified sections). The strategic freight network will also need to be electrified to provide the ability for most freight trains to operate under electric traction. The GBRTT is currently predicting that half of the UK's trains will be electric powered (some being battery electric) by 2050[13] but this also means that a significant number of trains will be powered by other sources, so research and development will need to continue on a number of fronts.

With an increased level of electrification, there should also be a larger proportion of the rail workforce and supply chain with the skills, capacity and relevant expertise to build, maintain and renew OLE. This has been an issue in the past for some countries. For example, in Great Britain, the electrification programme to date has been in fits and starts rather than being a continuous programme (West Coast Main Line in the 1960s and 1970s, East Coast Main Line in the 1980s, followed by very little activity until the last three or four years). On the other hand, Germany has been undertaking a steady electrification programme over many decades, maintaining a good level of expertise which itself maintains a lower cost base. Any 'boom and bust' cycle is detrimental to the supply chain as teams and people are lost during the gaps and have to be brought back later at a much higher cost to the industry.

2.3 Battery technology and hybrid trains

Battery technology provides an alternative to diesel for sections of the rail network that are not currently (or may never be) electrified. This involves either retrofitting existing rolling stock or designing new rolling stock with onboard batteries, which can be charged either while running on electrified sections of the route, or at stationary charging facilities.

While this technology is currently at the heart of the journey to decarbonisation of the road vehicle sector, through the roll out of electric vehicles (EVs) (see Chapter III), there are substantial limitations to its application in the rail sector. Current battery technology does not provide the power output required for freight or high-speed services – to produce the required amount of power would require a battery far too large to fit onto the train. Another key limiting factor is the relatively short distance battery-powered trains can travel before the battery needs to be recharged.

It is expected that charging technology will have advanced considerably with induction charging (which does not need a physical connection between the battery and the charging point) and direct contact by a pantograph onto a section of OLE or charging bar catenary (a fixed bar above the tracks similar to a short section of OLE at a station or depot). Important factors in the chosen method of recharging will be the speed and efficiency of the charging system and the frequency at which the charging can take place.

Given the power outputs and the range of battery trains, it is likely that they will be better suited to those parts of the rail network which require lower speed trains and where the level of services required do not justify the investment of expensive OLE equipment. A metro service using short, frequent, recharging at most stations along its route would work well with battery power and avoid the need for an expensive OLE system, particularly if a new urban route is required as part of a city's expanding public transport network.

Due to the excessive draw of power required to start heavy freight trains, battery power is best suited to passenger trains, but as well as pure battery power, a battery can be particularly useful in extending the range of other power sources. These are typically 'hybrids' capable of switching between battery and another form of power, such as overhead lines (with the battery being charged up when the train is running on the electrified sections) or diesel/biofuels. There are also examples of tri-mode trains which can switch between battery, electricity and diesel modes (eg, Hitachi Rail has recently launched 20 tri-mode (or 'tribrid') trains in Italy).

Although battery trains are emission free at the point of operation, a large amount of energy is used during their production and disposal of batteries, which given their relatively short lifespan (typically five to 15 years at the time of writing) means that the 'embodied carbon' in the battery needs to be accounted for several times during the train's lifecycle.

One significant disadvantage of using battery power are the concerns around battery production and disposal. Although battery trains are emission free at the point of operation, a large amount of energy is used during their production and disposal of batteries, which given their relatively short lifespan (typically five to 15 years at the time of writing) means that the 'embodied carbon' in the battery needs to be accounted for several times during the train's lifecycle.

Batteries also require significant quantities of rare metals and there is likely to be considerable competition for these by 2050. As such, these prices may affect the affordability of battery trains compared to other power sources. A combination of power sources using hybrids is likely to be the more common use of batteries in the rail sector rather than using battery-only trains.

2.4 Hydrogen

Hydrogen is another way of powering trains as an alternative to diesel on non-electrified lines, although it is currently at an early stage of adoption in the rail sector. This technology uses on board fuel cells that convert hydrogen and oxygen into electricity through an electrochemical reaction, emitting water vapour and heat as by-products.

An advantage of hydrogen is that it is more efficient at converting the power into electricity compared to battery-powered trains meaning hydrogen fuel cell trains have a much longer range than battery-powered trains. In the UK, train manufacturer Alstom and train owner/financier Eversholt Rail have developed the 'Breeze' hydrogen train, which is converted from existing rolling stock, and Porterbrook has developed and tested the 'HydroFLEX' hydrogen train,[14] although neither is yet in service in the UK. Elsewhere, hydrogen-powered trains are being ordered and/or trialled in a number of countries (including the US, Japan, Italy, Namibia, India and China).

Another advantage of hydrogen is that if electrification of a route is not available (potentially due to the high cost of installation/maintenance compared to revenue generated by that line), then it provides an effectively zero carbon solution for local and rural services. Hydrogen trains are arguably best used where there is a ready source of hydrogen available nearby, whether that is as a by-product from a chemical plant or another easily accessible source, such as hydrogen production plant for a local bus network.

However, there are disadvantages. A key issue with hydrogen relates to production of the hydrogen itself. Currently only a small proportion of hydrogen is produced using renewable energy sources to electrolyse water (so-called 'green hydrogen') and this method is expensive. Other cheaper methods of production produce GHGs in the process, undermining the role of hydrogen in achieving net zero. Hydrogen fuel cells are also expensive to produce. These issues mean there have been some setbacks in the commercial roll out of this technology. For example, LVNG, the state-owned railway company of Lower Saxony in Germany started running 14 hydrogen fuel cell-powered trains (Alstom Coradia iLint trains) on certain routes in Lower Saxony in August 2022, but less than a year later concluded that they would not be adopting the technology more widely due to high costs.

Another major downside of using hydrogen to power rail vehicles is the volumes of hydrogen required to be converted into electricity in the fuel cell and the levels of electricity that can be produced and effectively turned into tractive effort. Most of the trials for hydrogen trains have used multiple-unit passenger trains which have remained relatively close to the hydrogen fuel supply, meaning that only a limited amount of hydrogen has needed to be carried on the trains. The trains themselves have also been relatively lightweight when compared to a large intercity passenger train or heavy freight locomotive.

Large, heavy vehicles require significant amounts of power to be generated to overcome the frictional forces and create momentum. However, generating such high amounts of power from hydrogen is difficult. Hydrogen works relatively efficiently when the train to be moved is reasonably light but not when it is long and heavy. This is also a conclusion reached within the road sector, hence the continued development for buses but limited research in using hydrogen to power HGVs. A further concern is the effective energy cost in using electricity to create hydrogen and then using the hydrogen to create electricity. If OLE systems are available, electric trains would be a better solution and if there is a mix of OLE and unelectrified lines, an electric hybrid train would provide a more practicable solution.

Of all possible technologies to power rail vehicles, hydrogen arguably has one of the longer paths to travel before the technology can be rolled out on a commercial scale. However, it also has some of the least expensive infrastructure changes needed to support it – particularly when compared to electric or battery-powered trains. It is likely to have some success for shorter distance metro-type services, particularly if the hydrogen used is a genuine by-product of chemical processes near to that part of the rail network. Getting the right financial model will be key when competing against other technologies which are also very low carbon at point of use.

In addition to using a fuel cell process to convert hydrogen to electricity, engineers are also looking at the opportunities and benefits of using hydrogen as a combustion fuel within a converted diesel engine. This is covered in more detail in section 2.5(c) below.

2.5 Combustible fuels

(a) Enhanced diesel fuels

Work is progressing on developing enhanced diesel fuels (with a lower carbon content) and on aviation fuels (which are also primarily hydrocarbons). It is likely that some form of hydrocarbon aviation fuel will remain required because of the technology of aero jet engines. More on this can be found in Chapter VII.

Given the need for diesel-like power when a freight train is not on part of the electrified network, a solution which significantly reduces the carbon footprint without any major changes to the engine and little additional infrastructure (save for relevant fuel storage facilities) becomes financially viable. The questions will then be how politically acceptable such a solution would be compared to the cost of alternative lower-carbon solutions.

An advantage of biofuels is that they do not always require costly adaptions to rolling stock – they can be used in existing diesel engines and using the same refuelling mechanisms.

(b) Biofuels

Biofuels can also be used to reduce carbon emissions in the rail sector. Biofuels are made from organic matter such as vegetable oil, and although they do produce carbon dioxide (CO_2) emissions, levels are much lower compared to conventional diesel. An advantage of biofuels is that they do not always require costly adaptions to rolling stock – they can be used in existing diesel engines and using the same refuelling mechanisms.

Examples of use of biofuels in the rail sector include Germany's Prignitzer Eisenbahn which has been using biofuels since 2006, and Deutsche Bahn which in 2022 switched 57 regional trains to biofuel (hydrotreated vegetable oil) as part of a plan to phase out conventional diesel. Biofuels can also be blended with conventional diesel fuels to produce lower CO_2 emissions.

However, as with the other technologies, there are disadvantages to biofuels, including potential air quality issues. But the main obstacle to the adoption of biofuels in the rail sector is likely to be their availability. In its 2020 Traction Decarbonisation Network Strategy, Network Rail concludes that biofuel is "not a credible solution to decarbonise rail traction" in Great Britain due to availability issues.[15] There is a limit to how much biofuel can be produced as it competes with food production, and it is currently assumed that the production of biofuels is most likely to be prioritised for use in other transport modes such as aviation where there are few other credible alternatives.

(c) Hydrogen as a combustible fuel

Engineers are currently looking at the potential to use hydrogen as a combustion fuel within a converted diesel engine. Such a process will require the retrofitting of equipment to a traditional diesel engine in order to adapt the engine to use hydrogen as a fuel, but with a limited amount of change required to the existing power system itself.

The intention is to retain the physical benefits of using the existing diesel engines to create the electricity at sufficient levels to provide the power to start a heavy standing train. Given the problems in producing the required levels of power from a fuel cell compared to that from a diesel combustion engine, particularly for freight locomotives, this is a very interesting step. The project is in its early stages, but if successful could create a significant shift in the potential to use hydrogen for freight trains and a new dynamic in the presumed share of low carbon power sources in the rail sector.

2.6 A summary of relative advantages and disadvantages

Technology	Advantages	Disadvantages/ challenges
Electrified network (overhead lines or third rail)	• High efficiency, performance and reliability • Existing tried and tested technology • Can power freight and high-speed trains	• Significant cost and time required to upgrade network infrastructure • Installation work requires network closures • Electricity not fully generated by renewables • Damage to infrastructure prevents use of the power system
Battery (and hybrid)	• Suitable for electrified and non-electrified lines • Low capital cost compared to electrification • Inherent ability to replace batteries allows advances in battery technology to be introduced more quickly	• Short range • Long charging time • Heavy weight • Battery production and disposal issues • Not powerful enough for freight or high-speed trains
Hydrogen	• Longer range than battery • Fast refuelling • Can use by-products from chemical industry	• High cost • Most hydrogen production not zero emission • Not enough power output for freight or high-speed trains • Large volumes required for longer journeys
Diesel alternatives (including biofuel)	• Requires limited modification to existing rolling stock and facilities • Ability to provide a high-power output when required – particularly for freight trains	• Not zero emission • Prioritisation of biofuel for other modes (eg, aviation)

3. How do we get there?

3.1 Managing materials

Alongside the changes to power systems in the road to net zero are the construction materials being used for the new trains and relevant infrastructure. A lighter-weight train is likely to provide the opportunity to use a number of alternative power supplies but there is a balance to be struck between using construction materials which have a lower carbon footprint and retaining sufficient strength in the newer materials to provide the required levels of crashworthiness in the vehicles. Material science may allow vehicles to become lighter and use less energy to power them while still having the same strength, but given the weight of either the passengers or the freight that they are carrying, there will reach a point where small changes in the materials will have a limited effect.

The railway infrastructure will also need to change, regardless of the alternative fuels which are chosen. Net zero will need to take account of the carbon footprint of the materials used – whether that is for the construction of new OLE designed to withstand the effects of climate change or hydrogen storage and refuelling equipment. Getting the right balance between cost, robustness and safety will have an influence on which solution is appropriate for any section of railway line, given that few countries are likely to have an unlimited budget to go down a single solution route such as full electrification. In this area the safety and standards body such as the UK's RSSB will play an important part and is why, in the UK context, RSSB is an appropriate body to be the facilitator of the Sustainable Rail Blueprint.

3.2 Electrification

The technology for power systems in electric trains has been available for many years and cost-effective systems are readily available off the shelf from all major rolling stock manufacturers. This means that technological advancements are generally relatively small, although changes in the construction of pantographs for collecting the power from the overhead line and the efficiency of the electric motors can bring about costs savings which can have a real difference when looking at the whole life cost of the trains.

For a fully electric train, the main constraint on its use is the extent of the electrified network it is running on. Whenever there is a break in this network, the train is unable to collect electricity to continue to power the train. However, the train does continue to run under its own momentum, and it is possible to use batteries which can provide both drive and auxiliary services such as train lighting and WiFi services for a period of time. This means that if there is a short break in the OLE, such as where there is a low bridge or short tunnel which would be very expensive to alter, the train can continue to operate. The key here is to ensure that the pantograph technology for collecting the power from the OLE is able to manage the gaps which occur in the OLE wires. Technology is already being developed to manage the effects of pantographs crossing such gaps in the OLE wires.

In producing fully electric trains, consideration needs to be given to the infrastructure that they will need to draw their power from. OLE systems are extremely expensive to construct, and research is currently being undertaken to look at simpler and cheaper systems for lower speed routes. Trials are currently being proposed for power supply systems for rural routes and specific freight routes which cannot justify the expense of a full OLE system. These include lighter weight masts suitable for lower speeds and systems similar to those used on tramways.

A key piece of equipment is the pantograph which takes the power from the OLE. For a rural service which will just run under the lower cost OLE, the pantograph would simply need to be compatible with the lower cost OLE. A freight locomotive which would need to use both types of OLE would either need to have a single pantograph capable of operating on both systems or potentially two different pantographs which could be deployed dependent on the type of OLE being used. Ideally having a single pantograph would be best to avoid the complexities of changing the pantograph during a journey but a trade-off would be needed between the cost and practical application of different pantographs and the installation and maintenance costs of any low-cost OLE system.

3.3 Battery and hybrid

Battery technology continues to be developed and several trials of this technology are ongoing. The level of investment in developing this technology is much greater in the road sector than in rail, but there is no major barrier to rail trialling the technology that has been developed for road vehicles, particularly HGVs, for its trains. The key points are to have a sufficiently large amount of electricity being delivered to the motors to make the wheels move even with a heavy load and for the battery to contain enough electricity to allow the vehicle to complete its required operations before being recharged.

While battery manufacturers are creating better batteries, particularly with respect to energy stored within the battery, its charging rate and operational life, the train vehicle manufacturers are working to develop the next generation of battery trains which are lighter, have better aerodynamics and a more efficient use of the power load on the battery. Projects are ongoing to look at ways of minimising the weight of trains through articulation (two vehicles sharing one bogie), using

Trials are currently being proposed for power supply systems for rural routes and specific freight routes which cannot justify the expense of a full OLE system. These include lighter weight masts suitable for lower speeds and systems similar to those used on tramways.

composite materials which do not compromise crashworthiness (while also reducing embedded carbon) and using the best power-to-weight battery packs.

Minimising other drains on the battery's power are also being investigated. Modern trains have air conditioning systems, WiFi packages and lighting which also use electricity. Work is therefore needed to produce efficient systems which require less power to operate, and these are already coming on stream alongside the new generation of battery trains. In addition to the level of the auxiliary load, the ambient temperature may also have an effect on the level of charge produced by the battery.

A number of trials of battery trains have seen battery units used to replace the existing power systems of older passenger trains which have been retired from service. Potentially the most successful to date have been the class 230 trains which have the added benefit of reusing ex-London Underground District Line stock. The lightweight nature of these trains makes them ideal for battery power and the linked development of a fast-charging technology is a significant aspect of their appeal to operators.[16]

How the vehicle can be recharged will be a factor in any EV's availability. Early trials used cables attached to lineside charging points to provide a direct charge while latterly there has been an increase in research on induction charging which does not need the physical connection between train and charging point. Other proposals have been looking at the ability to recharge the battery from power taken from an OLE where the battery train runs into a station platform which also has OLE running above the tracks. Currently, the UK's DfT is sponsoring a number of 'first-of-a-kind' proposals looking at battery train charging stations.[17]

An alternative technology, which is already providing popular in parts of the light rail sector is using a fast static charging system. A fixed bar catenary is used at the vehicle's terminus (and at intermediate stations for longer routes) which can be accessed by the vehicle's pantograph. Automatic power charging takes place while the vehicle is stationary, and the system turns off when the pantograph is lowered. Current research on test trains show that a full charge can be obtained within 10 minutes of beginning the charging cycle, while recharging at intermediate stations can take place while passengers get on and off the vehicles in order to top up the battery.[18]

As battery technology advances, the ability to use battery as the secondary power source will increase, but GBRTT is currently predicting that a number of diesel and diesel bi-modes will still be operating in 2050.

With a number of power systems becoming available, current development for hybrid passenger trains is focusing on an electric-battery combination. However, for freight services and heavy long distance passenger trains, the concern is that using battery as the secondary traction source will not provide sufficient power (particularly when starting a heavy freight train where there is no OLE) and a diesel engine (or alternative combustible fuel) will be required. In some cases, particularly for freight locomotives, it may be possible to have three different power sources: (i) electric for when running on an electrified system; (ii) diesel when hauling a freight train on an unelectrified track; and (iii) batteries for simple movements of the locomotive when not connected to wagons where it does not need to sheer power offered by electric or diesel traction.

An issue for any hybrid train is the additional space taken up by the secondary power unit. Systems which require a small fuel tank due to the energy density of the fuel are likely to be favoured over others which require a large fuel tank due to low energy density (such as for hydrogen). As battery technology advances, the ability to use battery as the secondary power source will increase, but GBRTT is currently predicting that a number of diesel and diesel bi-modes will still be operating in 2050.[19]

3.4 Hydrogen

Arguably one of the least well-developed propulsion systems at present is using hydrogen. Electric, battery and combustible fuel systems have been used for many years although the drive to decarbonisation has caused the industry to revisit how they are used and to consider what technological developments can be carried out to make them more efficient and cost effective. Hydrogen fuel cells really are the new technology coming to the rail sector and, as a result, a large number of train manufacturers are investing in research projects in order to develop and then exploit the technology.

The large numbers of trials being undertaken in the UK and elsewhere – both by train leasing companies and train manufacturers – is likely to mean that the technology moves forward faster than those of battery or alternative combustible fuels. The rail sector is also taking careful note of developments in hydrogen power in road vehicles, especially buses (more details of which can be found in Chapter III).

If the ongoing development of hydrogen fuel cells results in systems that can produce energy faster and in greater amounts than they can currently achieve, then hydrogen may be able to displace battery on certain routes. Managing the on-train storage of hydrogen in sufficient quantities will be a significant factor in how well hydrogen fares as a power source in 2050. While it is possible to store larger amounts of hydrogen at high pressure, this creates significant risks. The potential for using high-pressure hydrogen and the benefits for net zero (including the cost of providing such form of hydrogen power) must be considered in the light of any accident involving the train and its potential for harm to passengers and others compared to the costs and benefits of alternative power sources.

3.5 Combustible fuels

The interest in biofuels from the late 1990s and early 2000s has been reignited more recently and research into using biofuels has been stepped up, particularly where the fuel is obtained by recycling other products. Various projects are looking at the level of biofuel which can be mixed with existing diesel fuel[20] while others are looking at using biofuels made from waste and residuals of raw materials which provide a replacement for diesel.[21] This research is primarily supported by the rail freight sector to provide a lower carbon substitute for diesel where the freight routes they use do not have OLE.

In the area of combustible fuels, hydrogen may just have an opportunity of breaking into the freight sector as research is starting into using hydrogen as a combustible fuel within a converted diesel engine. Iarnród Éireann (Irish Railways) has recently begun an experimental project with Latvian company DIGAS to design, produce, install, test and commission equipment for operating a combustion engine with hydrogen.[22] The intention is to produce a locomotive which is capable of running with a hydrogen internal combustion engine (H2 ICE) and to create retro-fit kits which allow existing diesel engines to be converted to running on renewable, emission free hydrogen. The benefits of such a system would be that in addition to the zero carbon fuel, the existing diesel engines (which include a reasonably significant amount of embedded carbon) can be re-used creating a sustainable environmentally friendly solution.

Depending on the outcomes of the trials, a conversion kit for existing diesel engines could be a significant breakthrough. Questions on the storage of sufficient fuel would still need to be met, but the opportunity to continue to use locomotives which still have a significant number of years of serviceable life within them would provide a cost-effective solution to operators, lessors and manufacturers.

4. Reducing carbon in the supporting infrastructure for new power systems

4.1 Infrastructure to support rolling stock power supplies

While the majority of power systems for rolling stock are to a large degree self-contained within the vehicle itself, arguably the most efficient of all, the continuous electricity supply system, requires a significant amount of infrastructure outside of the vehicle in order for the vehicle to be powered.

(a) Getting to grips with overhead electric line installation

To date the UK's railways have had an uneasy relationship with cost effective installation of OLE. The last major electrification in England and Wales, the Great Western Main Line to Swansea (undertaken between 2010 and 2017), saw the project terminated early due to spiralling costs. The electrified section only reached Cardiff and the additional lines up to Oxford and through Bath to Bristol were never built. Costs were estimated at approximately £4 million per single track kilometre. Since then, however, there has been ongoing electrification works in Scotland, where costs have been reduced to £1.2 million per single track kilometre. This is higher though than the average costs in Germany and Denmark which are at £1 million per single track kilometre, so there remains room for the UK to become more efficient and cost effective at rolling out electric infrastructure.[23]

Some of the issues which increase the cost of installing OLE in the UK are brought about by the size of the infrastructure and the work necessary to produce a safe operating height for the OLE system. As one of the first countries in the world to build commercial railways,

While the majority of power systems for rolling stock are to a large degree self-contained within the vehicle itself, arguably the most efficient of all, the continuous electricity supply system, requires a significant amount of infrastructure outside of the vehicle in order for the vehicle to be powered.

the common design size, or 'loading gauge' for the UK ended up being smaller than that established for a number of European railways. There is often less flexibility when installing overhead lines in the UK meaning that more work (and consequently more cost) has been incurred when lines have been electrified. In addition, the stop-start process of electrification has meant that there is a lack of skilled OLE engineers with limited experienced to call upon which itself drives up costs.

If trains are being pulled by a purely electric locomotive, the OLE needs to provide a continuous line for the train to draw power from. However, by adding a battery into the power system of an electric train there is an alternative power supply available for a short section of track which does not have OLE above it, allowing the train to continue to operate until the next set of OLE is reached. This use of discontinuous electrification means that expensive replacement works for a bridge or re-gauging a short tunnel can be avoided.

Technology is still being developed to manage the pantograph detaching and re-attaching to the line as the OLE ends and restarts, the safe operating speeds for doing so and the length of gap that the train can safety traverse. However, being able to exploit the benefits of this type of infrastructure can potentially bring the benefits of electrification to a much wider section of the rail network.

(b) Providing battery charging points

The available time to recharge a battery is a significant factor in the effectiveness of battery locomotives. If there is due to be a reasonable amount of time in a lay-over at the end of a journey, a more 'standard' form of recharging point can be provided. Current practice is either for an induction plate between the rails (such as for class 220) or for a cable to be physically attached to the train.

If there is less time available, then a fast-charging induction system placed between the rails can be used, provided that there is a sufficiently powerful electrical connection to the national grid. However, gaining access to a sufficiently high-powered section of the national grid and laying in new cables to provide such a charge may be prohibitively expensive, particularly at the end of branch line. Understanding the best points to link into the relevant part of the national grid will be a key factor in affecting the financial suitability for battery power of a particular section of network.

While the technology in power systems continues to develop, some of the more mundane physical issues will also need to be solved. This could include the infrastructure provider installing its own power distribution system alongside the railway (rather than having cables

The technology to store and load hydrogen onto trains has been progressing rapidly during the past decade. A significant amount of work has been undertaken within the bus industry, where hydrogen is a target alternative fuel to diesel, and much of this can be applied to the rail sector.

suspended from masts) and linking into specific battery recharging points at positions which suit railway operations, rather than being reliant on the recharging at places best suited for access to the national grid.

(c) Hydrogen storage and loading

The technology to store and load hydrogen onto trains has been progressing rapidly during the past decade. A significant amount of work has been undertaken within the bus industry, where hydrogen is a target alternative fuel to diesel, and much of this can be applied to the rail sector.

To date the main tests have been carried out on converted multiple units which are relatively lightweight, requiring similar amounts of hydrogen as have been used in the bus trials. It is unlikely that the refuelling systems will undergo significant change as between rail and bus and the main difference going forward is likely to be in the size of the storage facility. However, given that the chemical industry has managed the storage of significant volumes of hydrogen for many years it is not expected that much technological change will be required to off-the-shelf infrastructure required to support hydrogen-powered trains.

(d) Biofuel provision

The advantage of biofuels is that they can be stored in lineside facilities and pumped into locomotives in a similar manner to diesel fuel. Similar safety requirements to those for diesel fuel are expected to apply to the storage facilities and in respect of the equipment used to replenish fuel tanks on the locomotives.

It is also possible to provide fuel from road tankers which can be parked next to the locomotive. These mobile storage points remove the need for expensive underground or surface mounted storage tanks and are arguably more suitable to freight locomotives which operate into quarries and freight yards and potentially have limited times during a shift pattern when they may return to a depot for refuelling. They have been developed to enable trials in alternative biofuels to take place and benefit of these tankers is still being assessed.

It should be noted that existing diesel trains could be fuelled from road tankers but historically refuelling has always taken place at a depot where there are greater safety provisions, particularly to manage fuel spillages and leakages. To the extent that there are smaller fleets of locomotives using biofuels as their power source, consideration should

Most civil engineers now have carbon reduction targets which they are being required to meet. An amount of this reduction can be achieved through the design of the railway and the methods and materials used in the construction of new infrastructure.

be given to how the refuelling provisions work. The requirements for providing large underground storage tanks may no longer be needed and the environmental risk be better managed through supplying fuels at designated sites from smaller surface mounted tanks.

4.2 Decarbonising civil engineering

(a) Managing carbon in construction, maintenance and renewals

It is not just the trains and their operations where the UK needs to look at decarbonisation. The infrastructure that the trains run on contributes a significant amount of carbon emissions to the rail sector. This is particularly true for the steel used for the OLE supports, and in the concrete used for bridges, tunnels and other buildings which need to be altered to support the new net zero power sources.

Most civil engineers now have carbon reduction targets which they are being required to meet. An amount of this reduction can be achieved through the design of the railway and the methods and materials used in the construction of new infrastructure. HS2 Limited have reported that of their carbon footprint for Phase One of HS2, construction materials account for 49% of carbon emissions, transporting those materials 11%, actual construction 13%, maintenance and replacement of those materials over their life 13% and operational energy 14%.[24]

Questions can be asked of a system's designers and traditional designs can be altered to reduce the physical amounts of building materials in a structure, whether that is steel, concrete or other building materials. In some cases, it is possible to reduce the amount of material through a change of design while in others, using a different specification of a material can achieve a carbon reduction. However, the search for a lower carbon, greater strength material needs to be balanced by the cost of that material and alternative ways of making the relevant carbon saving.

A carbon offsetting process can also be put in place to ensure that there is an overall carbon net zero effect for the combined construction, maintenance and renewals activities for that infrastructure. The long-life nature of rail's civil assets means that carbon offsetting may not be 100% at day one, but properly managed plantations have the ability to create a net carbon saving benefit over the medium to longer term.

When it comes to replacing an infrastructure asset, thought should be given as to how best to use the embedded carbon within that asset. Given that just under half of the carbon footprint of infrastructure assets comes from obtaining the construction materials themselves, options for recycling the asset should be considered. Where the content of the asset being replaced may be used outside of the rail industry, carbon credits should be sought so that the benefits can continue to be obtained by the rail sector.

(b) Reducing carbon in steel

Most of the world's major steelmakers are continuing research into production methods which allow a reduction in the levels of carbon in rails. This includes using electric arc furnaces to produce recycled steel which can then be used for a number of applications within the rail sector.

This low carbon, high sustainability solution is already in use by the Belgian railway infrastructure manager, Infrabel, which received its first batch of 'green rails' in May 2023. Infrabel is expecting to reduce its carbon emissions by approximately 224,000 tonnes during an initial four-year period.[25]

(c) Managing carbon in concrete

Decarbonisation has seen a drive within the construction industry to reduce the carbon footprint of concrete. Various methods have been developed to reduce carbon in concrete, particularly with respect to making blended mixes using limestone, slag or fly ash. The rail sector is able to benefit from this work without the need for much rail-specific research. A number of new standards for concrete are being produced and made available via national bodies such as the National Ready Mixed Concrete Association (NRMCA).[26]

In its January 2022 report, "Net Zero Carbon Plan: A cleaner, greener future", HS2 Limited provided a helpful insight into ways it was working to reduce the carbon footprint of its concrete usage.[27] In addition to trialling a new low carbon concrete product, HS2 Limited was piloting using recycled wind turbine blades to produce reinforcement bars for its concrete, reducing carbon emissions for reinforcement by up to 90%. It has also been using SD reinforced concrete printing onsite, which has resulted in a reduction of the quantities of concrete used by up to 50%. The reduction in concrete required has an additional benefit as it has meant that fewer deliveries of concrete have been needed, further reducing the anticipated amount of carbon associated with the transport sector.

5. Conclusion

Decarbonisation of the railways (and the methods used to build rail infrastructure) presents a significant opportunity to contribute to global efforts in reducing carbon emissions. The rail sector, when compared to road and aviation, already demonstrates a commendable track record of being a greener mode of transport with relatively low carbon emissions. However, there is still room for improvement to enhance rail's net zero credentials and further support the modal shift from road and aviation.

Electric powertrains are emerging as the frontrunner in green technology for the rail industry. Electrification of rail networks has shown promising results in reducing carbon emissions and improving energy efficiency. The widespread adoption of electric trains can significantly contribute to achieving net zero targets and further solidify rail's position as a sustainable mode of transportation.

Nevertheless, it is crucial to acknowledge that complete electrification is unlikely to be feasible or cost-effective for every rail network, particularly those covering very long distances or in challenging climates. In such cases, the exploration of alternative fuels and technologies, such as hydrogen or battery-powered trains, can play a pivotal role in reducing carbon emissions. By successfully replacing diesel-powered trains with these greener alternatives, wherever practicable, the rail sector can make substantial progress towards reaching net zero targets. Furthermore, the continued support and investment in research and development are essential to drive innovation and find sustainable solutions for the rail industry. Collaboration between governments, rail operators, and technology providers is vital to accelerate the adoption of greener technologies and ensure a successful transition towards a decarbonised rail sector.

The potential to use a number of the technologies being developed by the rail sector for other transport modes, as well as rail looking to other technological developments elsewhere is a key part of driving all forms of transport to net zero faster. Developments should not be contained within modal silos.

In summary, the decarbonisation of railways not only builds upon the sector's existing green credentials but also presents an opportunity to further reduce carbon emissions through modal shift and the adoption of greener technologies. By embracing electrification, exploring alternative fuels, and fostering innovation, the rail industry can play a pivotal role in achieving global climate goals and creating a more sustainable future for transportation.

Notes

1 Rail Safety and Standards Board, "Sustainable Rail Blueprint: The industry-wide blueprint for realising sustainable rail", p9, www.rssb.co.uk/-/media/Project/RSSB/RssbWebsite/Documents/Public/Public-content/Sustainability/the-sustainable-rail-blueprint.pdf?_gl=1*tcit9w*_ga*MjcxNzY4NTYzLjE3MjAwODQxMzQ.*_ga_TXMTJKV7TY*MTcyMDA4NDEzNC4xLjEuMTcyMDA4NDI3OS4wLjAuMA.

2 Department for Transport (DfT), "Rail Environment Policy Statement: On Track for a Cleaner, Greener Railway", July 2021, https://assets.publishing.service.gov.uk/media/60eee7498fa8f50c7f08ae4b/rail-environment-policy-statement.pdf.

3 *Ibid.*

4 DfT, "Decarbonising Transport: A Better, Cleaner Britain", 2021,

https://assets.publishing.service.gov.uk/media/610d63ffe90e0706d92fa282/decarbonising-transport-a-better-greener-britain.pdf.
5 Rail Minister, Jo Johnson: Speech to Knowledge Quarter Conference, British Museum, 12 February 2018, see www.gov.uk/government/speeches/lets-raise-our-ambitions-for-a-cleaner-greener-railway.
6 Transport Scotland, "Rail Services Decarbonisation Action Plan", July 2020, www.transport.gov.scot/media/47906/rail-services-decarbonisation-action-plan.pdf.
7 Network Rail, "Traction Decarbonisation Network Strategy: Interim Programme Business Case", 31 July 2020, www.networkrail.co.uk/wp-content/uploads/2020/09/Traction-Decarbonisation-Network-Strategy-Interim-Programme-Business-Case.pdf.
8 Rail Safety and Standards Board (RSSB), "The Sustainable Rail Blueprint", 11 November 2023, www.rssb.co.uk/sustainability/the-sustainable-rail-blueprint.
9 *Ibid*, p7.
10 The Rail Social Value Tool is an RSSB-developed online tool which can be used to monitor and measure the social value of projects and day-to-day operations in order to guide investment decisions, see www.rssb.co.uk/sustainability/maximising-social-value/the-rail-social-value-tool.
11 Examples include countries such as Germany, France, Sweden and China.
12 Mott Macdonald presentation: "Increasing the use of batteries – where are they in operation and how can they best be used?", Achieving Rail Decarbonisation conference (20 September 2023).
13 GBRTT presentation: "Delivering a more sustainable and greener railway – a long-term strategy with near term actions", Achieving Rail Decarbonisation conference (20 September 2023).
14 The first HydroFLEX train was developed in partnership with the University of Birmingham.
15 See n 7 above, p61, www.networkrail.co.uk/wp-content/uploads/2020/09/Traction-Decarbonisation-Network-Strategy-Interim-Programme-Business-Case.pdf.
16 Railway Technology, "GWR buys Vivarail's battery train-linked assets", 17 February 2023, www.railway-technology.com/news/gwr-vivarail-battery-train-assets/?cf-view.
17 DfT presentation: "Rail decarbonisation – it's a journey", Achieving Rail Decarbonisation conference (20 September 2023).
18 See n 12 above.
19 See n 13 above.
20 Railway Technology, "Cutting freight carbon emissions with biofuels", 12 May 2022, www.railway-technology.com/features/cutting-freight-carbon-emissions-with-biofuels/?cf-view.
21 Railtech.com, "DB reaches HVO biofuel target to years earlier", 13 January 2023, www.railtech.com/rolling-stock/2023/01/13/db-reaches-hvo-biofuel-target-two-years-earlier/#:~:text=The%20railway%20company%20has%20already,existing%20fleet%20will%20follow%20suit.
22 Railtech.com, "Irish Rail to trial Europe's first locomotive to combust hydrogen instead of diesel", 19 September 2023, www.railtech.com/innovation/2023/09/19/irish-rail-and-latvias-digas-to-trial-europes-first-retrofitted-hydrogen-freight-locomotive/.
23 RailEngineer, "Getting electrification right", 4 June 2018, www.railengineer.co.uk/getting-electrification-right/.
24 HS2, "Net Zero Carbon Plan: A cleaner, greener future", January 2022, p9, https://assets.hs2.org.uk/wp-content/uploads/2022/01/25357_HS2_NetZeroCarbonPlan_CS1656_Final_InteractiveWeb_Accessible.pdf.
25 Railtech.com, "Infrabel receives greener rails", 22 May 2023, www.railtech.com/innovation/2023/05/22/infrabel-receives-greener-rails/?gdpr=deny.
26 National Ready Mixed Concrete Association (NRMCA), "The top ten ways to reduce concrete's carbon footprint", www.nrmca.org/wp-content/uploads/2022/07/Top10WaysReduceConcreteCarbonFootprint.pdf.
27 See n 24 above, p12, https://assets.hs2.org.uk/wp-content/uploads/2022/01/25357_HS2_NetZeroCarbonPlan_CS1656_Final_InteractiveWeb_Accessible.pdf.

III. Zero and low emission road vehicles

Ellen Beardsworth
Paul Dight
Anna Sweeney
Addleshaw Goddard

1. Zero emission road vehicles

The days of the internal combustion engine (ICE) are numbered. To keep global temperature rises below 1.5°C the world needs to switch from polluting modes of transport to those with cleaner or no tailpipe emissions. The zero emission or electric vehicle (EV) has been one of the most important factors driving forward the green movement in transport and net zero ambitions in the automotive industry. Unlike traditional ICE vehicles that rely on fossil fuels, EVs operate solely on electricity stored in advanced battery systems. These vehicles produce zero tailpipe emissions, which in turn mitigates air pollution and reduces the overall carbon footprint associated with the vehicle as a mode of transport. Many countries have set, or are in the process of setting, targets and policies to phase-out ICE vehicles. These are mainly cars and (in some, but not all cases) light duty vehicles (vans).

2. Zero emission technology options

When we think of a zero emission vehicle (ZEV), the first thing that springs to mind is probably a battery-powered car. But this is not the only option and may not always be the most appropriate technology type for a particular use-case. It will depend on the size of the vehicle and how, or even where, it is used.

2.1 Electric battery technology

(a) Lithium-ion batteries

Lithium-ion batteries are the most widely adopted and recognised form of battery technology and most EVs are powered by lithium-ion batteries. While this technology has been around for decades, it is still developing and every year sees improved battery technology with increased power density allowing EVs to cover greater distances between charges, and the cost of such batteries is also reducing over time. That is not to say that battery technology is not without criticism. The biggest concern raised by some critics is the fact that while the technology is green at the tailpipe, the manufacturing process is carbon intensive and requires mining and use of scarce minerals like cobalt and lithium. In 2022, about 60% of global lithium demand was for EV batteries, along with 30% of cobalt and 10% of nickel demand; and lithium demand exceeded supply. We explore this further in section 5 below.[1]

(b) LFP batteries

Alternatives to lithium-ion batteries are emerging. Many Chinese original equipment manufacturers (OEMs) are using lithium iron phosphate (LFP) batteries, which contain iron and phosphorous rather than standard nickel, manganese and cobalt. At the time of writing, the Chinese OEM, BYD, accounts for 50% of the demand for LFP batteries, but Tesla is also increasing its use of LFP battery technology. The benefit of LFP batteries is that they use fewer scarce minerals, but the downside is their energy density is lower, meaning the distance an EV can travel between charges is shorter. LPF batteries also contain phosphorous, which is used in food production so there is a risk that this could lead to increased competition in the future for the same resources.

(c) Sodium-ion batteries

Sodium-ion (Na-ion) batteries are another alternative technology to lithium-ion. Sodium-ion batteries are cheaper than the alternatives and avoid the need for critical minerals. But again, they have a lower energy density than lithium-ion batteries, so are more suited for use in smaller and lighter cars and give a shorter range. BYD is building the world's largest sodium-ion battery factory and other automotive OEMs are starting to roll out sodium-ion battery-powered EVs, so we expect to see this market grow in the future.

(d) Solid-state batteries

Solid-state batteries are also being tested and could become commercially available shortly. They use solid electrodes and a solid electrolyte made up of ceramics, rather than the flammable liquid and polymer gel electrolytes used in conventional lithium batteries. As such they are theoretically safer as they are less prone to overheating and combustion – a significant criticism of the traditional lithium-ion battery. Solid-state batteries can reduce an EV's overall carbon footprint and have a higher energy density than lithium-ion batteries so once they become commercially available it is possible that they could become the go-to battery technology.

Ultimately, the financial – and environmental – cost of raw materials could well determine which battery technology becomes dominant in EV manufacture.

2.2 Charging of battery EVs

(a) Plug-in charging

There are several typical methods for charging EVs. Level 1 charging involves plugging the vehicle into a standard household electrical outlet using a charging cable provided with the EV. This method is convenient but slow, typically providing a charging rate of around two to five miles of range per hour of charging.

Level 2 charging requires the installation of a dedicated charging station or wall box. Level 2 chargers use a higher voltage and provide

Ultimately, the financial – and environmental – cost of raw materials could well determine which battery technology becomes dominant in EV manufacture.

a faster charging rate, typically ranging from 10 to 30 miles of range per hour of charging. These chargers are commonly found in public charging stations, workplaces and homes with dedicated EV wall boxes.

For even faster charging, there is Level 3 charging, also known as 'DC fast', 'rapid' or 'ultra-fast' charging. Level 3 chargers use direct current (DC) instead of alternating current (AC) and can provide a significant amount of charge in a short period. These chargers are typically found at public charging stations or charging 'hubs' and can provide up to 80% charge in 30 minutes or less, depending on the EV and the charger's capacity.

(b) Battery swapping

One of the hurdles to EV adoption is the concern over the duration of time needed to charge an EV as it takes longer than refuelling a petrol, diesel or hydrogen vehicle. One potential solution to overcome this is the concept of 'battery swapping'.

Battery swapping involves replacing the depleted battery with a fully charged one at a dedicated battery swapping station. In the same time it might take to refuel an ICE vehicle, and without having to get out of

One of the hurdles to EV adoption is the concern over the duration of time needed to charge an EV as it takes longer than refuelling a petrol, diesel or hydrogen vehicle. One potential solution to overcome this is the concept of 'battery swapping'.

the car, a driver could drive away with a fully charged battery. There could even be scope to replace a battery with a more powerful battery than the one swapped out if the driver was planning a long journey.

The cost of the battery makes up a large proportion of the overall cost of a battery EV. An advantage of the battery swap model is that the EV owner does not have to buy the battery in their vehicle outright. If the cost of such battery was removed from the purchase price of an EV, then the purchase price of the EV would be substantially reduced, making it a more competitive vehicle option. The EV owner would then pay a monthly subscription fee to use the battery swap service. This would, of course, need wide-scale adoption to work.

Swapping batteries also means the vehicle always has a battery that is optimised and does not degrade over time. This alleviates two main concerns of EV owners: range anxiety and the battery's cost and lifespan.

Battery swapping also has advantages over fast charging as it has less impact on the electricity grid because the batteries do not need to be charged as quickly and the batteries can also be used to store power from the grid at times of oversupply.

The speed of battery swapping makes it suited to public service vehicles such as buses and taxis, which would otherwise need to be recharged quickly while they are in use and could potentially offer more flexibility for route planning for less busy routes. It could also work well for private EV owners without access to a domestic charge point.

The main disadvantages are that battery swapping is not compatible with all vehicle types – at least not yet. At present the Chinese manufacturer Nio seems to be cornering the market with over 1,300 battery swap stations in China and plans for over 100 in Europe. Interoperability between vehicle types raises questions around the OEM warranty and whether a vehicle would need an expensive retrofit to make battery swapping work. The battery swap stations also take up more space than conventional chargers, although the Nio stations combine both. Battery swapping is particularly useful for buses, which are built specifically for a bus operator. The operator can specify what battery swapping capability they need their buses to have, and the space at its bus depot to include a swapping station and storage for spare batteries.

Battery swapping also works well for smaller two or three-wheeler vehicles and is gaining momentum in India in particular,[2] where Gogoro has partnered with Zypp Electric to deploy six battery swapping stations and 100 electric two-wheelers as part of a pilot project for 'last mile' deliveries in Delhi.

(c) Other charging methods

There are other charging methods that may be possible but are far less developed than the methods described above. These include conductive charging, catenary charging and wireless charging:

- Conductive charging requires an electrical contact on the vehicle to be in direct contact with a wire either overhead or on the ground. An extendable arm known as a 'pantograph' sits on top of the vehicle to connect it with an overhead wire (catenary charging); or sits below the vehicle connecting it to a rail embedded in the road (conductive charging). The infrastructure required means this form of charging may only be suitable for heavy good vehicles or buses using major roads.
- Wireless charging involves transferring power to the vehicle via inductive coils built into the road. This technology is an upscaled version of well understood solenoid charging technology used for many years on domestic products such as electric toothbrushes.

There are pros and cons to each of these. Such charging technologies would allow drivers to charge 'on-the-go' without needing to factor in time to stop and recharge. It also means vehicles can be lighter as they will not need such powerful, heavy batteries.

However, these schemes require significant investment in infrastructure either in the form of electricity lines above the road or within the road bed, and this will come at significant cost. This means the technology is only like to be deployed on key routes, so would result in less flexibility as to which routes vehicles dependant on this charging method can take. There will also need to be some level of standardisation or interoperability in vehicles to each technology (whether pantograph or solenoid) and this interoperability and compatibility must allow vehicles to move across borders. Standardisation would therefore be required internationally, and while it may be easier to decree across communities such as the EU, there is likely to be much inconsistency in approaches preferred and rate of adoption by different nations.

Germany has converted three sections of its road network with catenary lines developed by Siemens to test pantograph charging technology for heavy goods vehicles (HGVs). Most notable is the A5 motorway near Frankfurt which is considered one of the most polluted sections of road in the country, with 135,000 vehicles passing along it daily (14,000 of them being HGVs). Truck-builder Scania has provided pantograph-enabled HGVs to run along the routes. Similarly, Sweden has ambition to build its first e-motorway along a 13-mile section of the E20 motorway between Stockholm, Gothenburg and Malmo. It is not yet known whether the route will use catenary, conductive or inductive charging, but the country plans to have 3,000 km of electric road by 2045. Transport for London (TfL) has introduced pantograph charging for its electric buses in south London which enables them to 'top up' during the day rather than having to return to the depot.

2.3 Hydrogen fuel cells

Another promising alternative to battery EV technology is the hydrogen fuel cell vehicle (FCV). These vehicles harness the power of hydrogen gas to generate electricity, offering zero emissions at the tailpipe.

At the core of FCV technology lies a high-pressure tank that stores hydrogen fuel, which can be compressed or liquefied for efficient storage. The fuel cell stack, consisting of individual fuel cells, is the heart of the vehicle. Hydrogen from the storage tank is supplied to the anode side of the fuel cell stack, where it undergoes electrolysis, splitting into protons and electrons. The electrons are forced to travel

Another promising alternative to battery EV technology is the hydrogen fuel cell vehicle (FCV). These vehicles harness the power of hydrogen gas to generate electricity, offering zero emissions at the tailpipe.

through an external circuit, creating an electric current that powers the FCV's electric motor. Oxygen from the air is supplied to the cathode side of the fuel cell stack, where it combines with the protons and electrons, producing water vapor as the only emission. This environmentally friendly aspect of hydrogen cars makes them a promising alternative for cleaner mobility.

BMW-owned luxury car brand, Rolls-Royce, has announced it is considering hydrogen fuel cell technology as an alternative to battery EVs for the future of its product line.

FCVs typically have a longer driving range compared to battery EVs, providing more flexibility for longer journeys without the need for frequent recharging. The technology is suited to HGVs which travel long distances and would require large heavy batteries to achieve the same distances. Moreover, refuelling an FCV is quick and convenient, taking just a few minutes like traditional petrol or diesel cars. This eliminates concerns about long charging times that are present with battery EVs but of course requires suitable and conveniently located refuelling facilities.

While FCVs offer significant environmental benefits, there are challenges to overcome. The development of a hydrogen refuelling infrastructure is crucial to support widespread adoption. Currently, the number of hydrogen refuelling stations is limited, making it difficult for drivers to find convenient refuelling options. Indeed, the number of hydrogen refuelling stations in Britain has reduced from 10 in March 2022 to six in January 2024. This lack of infrastructure poses a barrier to the widespread adoption of hydrogen cars. Additionally, the production of hydrogen gas often involves energy-intensive processes, so the overall environmental impact depends on the carbon intensity of the hydrogen production.

The infrastructure required for hydrogen production, storage and transportation adds to the overall operating costs of FCVs, making FCVs typically more expensive than equivalent low- or zero-carbon vehicles.

2.4 Hybrid

The term 'hybrid' can refer to two types of vehicles: self-charging hybrids (HEVs) or plug-in hybrids (PHEVs):

- HEVs have a small battery and electric motor to supplement a petrol or diesel engine. The movement of the vehicle recharges the battery and the car can only drive a few miles using electric power alone.
- PHEVs also have a battery and electric motor, alongside a

Hybrid cars are arguably less fuel-efficient than standard petrol or diesel equivalents, as they are heavier due to having a battery and electric motor as well as an engine. They are generally viewed as a stepping stone between an ICE vehicle and a full battery EV.

(normally) petrol engine, but the battery is charged by plugging in to a charge point. This gives a range of around 25 to 55 miles in electric mode; great for short journeys, with the backup of a petrol engine for longer journeys.

Hybrid cars are arguably less fuel-efficient than standard petrol or diesel equivalents, as they are heavier due to having a battery and electric motor as well as an engine. They are generally viewed as a stepping stone between an ICE vehicle and a full battery EV.

As discussed in further detail in section 4 below, the United Kingdom is banning the sale of new hybrid cars and vans from 2035, as is the EU, so this market is likely to phase-out over time. In the meantime, however, sales of hybrids for use as taxis and private hire vehicles in the UK have increased in recent years due in large part to the imposition of clean air zones in various cities. Such clean air zones impose a charge to enter the zone on vehicles which exceed strict emissions criteria. One such example, the Ultra Low Emission Zone (ULEZ) in London, has led to taxis, private hire vehicles, buses and heavy goods vehicles switching to cleaner technologies, often with government support.

3. Impactful use cases

In addition to the private use of EVs by domestic consumers, there are two key applications for EVs that will have a significant contribution to achieving net zero targets by 2050: public transport and last mile delivery.

3.1 Public transport

Public transport in the UK is actively embracing electric and hydrogen vehicles as part of its commitment to a cleaner and more sustainable transportation system. Electric buses have become increasingly common in cities across the country. TfL, for example, operates a significant number of electric buses, contributing to reduced emissions and improved air quality in the UK's capital. The electrification of trains is also a priority, with various rail lines, including the London Overground, designed to accommodate electric trains. See Chapter II for more detail on rail decarbonisation.

In partnership with TfL, SSE is leading the world's largest vehicle-to-grid trial at a bus garage in London. Other partners also include the Mayor of London and Go-Ahead London. The trial is funded by the Department for Business, Energy and Industrial Strategy and the Office for Low Emission Vehicles, with support from Innovate UK. The three-

'Last mile' deliveries, the crucial final stage of the logistics supply chain, are undergoing significant transformations with the adoption of clean transport solutions which is reimagining how goods are transported to end customers.

year trial is part of a wider 'Bus2Grid' project which sees EVs charge not only their own batteries, but also feed excess energy back into the grid. It is anticipated that London, having a bus fleet of around 9,000 vehicles could theoretically provide enough energy to support 150,000 homes. The trial in London involves 28 double decker buses which would have the potential to feed 1MW of energy back into the grid.

Outside of London, Coventry is set to become the UK's first all-electric bus city. In 2022, Transport for West Midlands and Coventry City Council received £50 million of funding from the Department for Transport for the development of charging infrastructure and to upgrade fleets with EVs that will come under 'Coventry's Electric' programme.

Other forms of public transport vehicles are also being trialled, particularly hydrogen fuel cell buses, which are making advancements in the UK's public transport sector. Aberdeen stands out as a city that operates a fleet of hydrogen-powered buses, demonstrating the potential of hydrogen as a clean energy source.

3.2 'Last mile' deliveries

'Last mile' deliveries, the crucial final stage of the logistics supply chain, are undergoing significant transformations with the adoption of clean transport solutions which is reimagining how goods are transported to end customers.

One of the most notable changes in last mile deliveries is the increasing use of EVs. Logistics companies are shifting their fleets from traditional fossil fuel-powered vehicles to electric vans, bikes and scooters. Beyond the environmental benefits of EVs in general, these vehicles also offer lower operating costs and can be conveniently charged overnight at drivers' homes or at distribution centres when not in use – where vehicles are typically stored in any case.

EVs are then complemented by active transport modes such as bicycles, particularly in congested urban areas. These agile and cost-effective modes of transport offer emission-free operation, making them ideal for short-distance deliveries. Logistics companies are partnering with micro-mobility service providers or deploying their own fleet of micro-vehicles to navigate crowded city streets efficiently.

While it is not the focus of this chapter, it is noteworthy that the impact of switching last mile delivery transport modes to zero emission has been improved by the growing trend of delivery consolidation, where multiple packages from different retailers are grouped together for efficient delivery. By consolidating deliveries, fewer vehicles are needed, reducing emissions and alleviating congestion on the roads. This approach is facilitated by technology platforms that enable coordination and collaboration among retailers and logistics providers. All of this increases the ability of clean transport to help achieve net zero targets. Another innovation we are seeing in this market is the emergence of sharing platforms; allowing organisations to invest in charging either on a shared basis or offering others the opportunity to charge at their premises for a fee.

4. The legal imperative: the Zero Emission Vehicle Mandate

The UK has introduced a Zero Emission Vehicle (ZEV) Mandate on vehicle manufacturers requiring a minimum percentage of new car and van sales to be zero emission each year until 2035. The UK government initially committed to end the sale of new petrol and diesel cars and vans by 2030 and all non-ZEVs (ie, including hybrids) by 2035. It later revised the 2030 target back to 2035 but the ZEV Mandate means that 80% of new cars and 70% of new vans sold in Great Britain will need to be zero emission by 2030.

The ZEV Mandate evolved from a commitment in the UK government's Ten Point Plan of November 2020[3] to publish a Green Paper on a carbon dioxide (CO_2) regulatory framework for all new road vehicles in the UK. This Green Paper was published in July 2021 and proposed either tightening the existing efficiency-based regulations to more closely align with the UK's petrol and diesel phase-out commitments or making a UK ZEV mandate as well as CO_2 regulations.

In its response to the consultation in April 2022, the government decided to adopt a ZEV mandate and continue to regulate the CO_2 emissions of non-ZEVs to make sure they do not increase.

After further consultations,[4] the Vehicle Emissions Trading Scheme Order 2023[5] was made on 13 December 2023 and came into force on 3 January 2024. This implements four trading schemes relating to cars and vans registered in Great Britain (ie, not Northern Ireland, which remains subject to an adapted version of the existing regulations).

The four schemes create targets for zero emission car and van registrations which increase each year. This is done by way of allowances for non-ZEV registrations which reduce each year. The manufacturer must pay £15,000 per car and £9,000 (rising to £18,000 from 2025) per van registered above their annual allowance.

The regulations also require manufacturers to maintain an emissions target per vehicle (measured in grammes of CO_2 emitted per kilometre) equal to their 2021 target. So, if they manufacture more ICE cars and vans than they did in 2021, they must ensure that each vehicle emits less CO_2 overall or pay £86 per 1g of CO_2 emitted per kilometre above their target.

The UK has introduced a Zero Emission Vehicle (ZEV) Mandate on vehicle manufacturers requiring a minimum percentage of new car and van sales to be zero emission each year until 2035.

The European Union has introduced regulations[6] to set fleet-wide CO2 emission targets on car and van manufacturers for five-year periods culminating in zero emissions by 2035. These targets are coupled with an incentive mechanism for zero- and low-emission vehicles (ZLEVs), which allows a manufacturer's specific emission target to be relaxed by up to 5% if its proportion of new ZLEVs registered in a given year exceeds certain benchmarks.

There are already ZEV mandates in the United States, Canada and China. At the end of COP26 in 2021, various countries signed the Glasgow Declaration, now known as the ZEV Declaration;[7] a commitment to work towards all sales of new cars and vans being ZEVs by 2040 or earlier, or by no later than 2035 in leading markets. According to BloombergNEF, as at November 2022 there were 66 governments in total with an ICE phase-out target, including 20 national governments, 28 regional and municipal authorities and 18 additional EU countries which come under the EU's phase-out target.[8] These targets cover 41% of the global passenger vehicle market.

5. Challenges faced by the automotive industry

There are several challenges facing the automotive industry and the wide-spread adoption of ZEVs. We explore some of the key challenges in this section.

5.1 Changes in government policy

Historically, the UK government has expressed support for EVs as part of its commitment to reducing carbon emissions and addressing climate change. Policies have included financial incentives for EV buyers, grants for installing charging infrastructure and long-term plans to phase-out ICE vehicles.

However, opinions on policy constantly vary, and challenges have arisen in the implementation and continuity of such policies. Factors such as changes in government leadership, economic considerations and public opinion can influence the direction and consistency of policies related to EVs. For example, the recent shift in the requirement for all new ICEs to be phased out by 2030 was pushed back to 2035 by Prime Minister Rishi Sunak in September 2023. The justification was to reduce the financial impact on the consumer during the cost-of-living crisis. This changing in policy confuses the consumer. Those who were planning on changing their car in the next couple of years, for example, might have considered switching to an electric one. With an extra five years before the ban comes in, consumers are likely to simply wait for the next time they upgrade their car instead. Automotive OEMs will have already invested significantly in developing their ZEV product range and reducing

While the plug-in car grant is still available to EVs other than cars (eg, mopeds, vans and trucks) the government has instead chosen to direct its money towards encouraging charge point installation both publicly and domestically.

numbers of ICE vehicles manufactured. This change in direction could lead to OEMs having too much stock of products they cannot sell – which is significantly detrimental to the survival of the industry.

Similarly grants for buying an EV and for installing a domestic charge point have also either been phased-out or significantly decreased over time. For example, the plug-in car grant (introduced 2011) was closed to new car orders in June 2022, having previously been extended as recently as the Spring 2020 Budget. This grant previously gave purchasers up to £2,500 off the price of an EV costing less than £35,000 directly at the point of purchase. While the plug-in car grant is still available to EVs other than cars (eg, mopeds, vans and trucks) the government has instead chosen to direct its money towards encouraging charge point installation both publicly and domestically. The current incentives are discussed further below at section 6.4 below.

5.2 Environmental credentials of EV batteries

While an EV will produce no exhaust emissions and can be charged using renewable generated electricity, there are a number of criticisms levelled at EV adoption. A common criticism of EVs is that while they are zero emission at the tailpipe, the full lifecycle of an EV is not as environmentally friendly.

According to McKinsey, producing the lithium-ion batteries that power EVs accounts for around 40%–60% of total production emissions for the vehicle.[9] The mining and refining processes for the metals used in the batteries, like lithium and cobalt, are energy- and water-intensive.

Assessing the overall environmental impact of EV batteries involves considering the entire lifecycle, from raw material extraction to manufacturing, use and end-of-life management. Two key reasons for this are as follows:

- *Material sourcing and mining practices:* Battery production involves the extraction of raw materials. The mining and refining process for the metals used in the batteries, like lithium, nickel and cobalt, are energy- and water-intensive. They also raise environmental and social impact concerns – for example, where they disrupt wildlife habitats or cause soil erosion or pollution, and where the mining takes place in countries that use child labour or exploit and aggravate poverty. Companies and governments are increasingly focusing on responsible sourcing practices to minimise negative effects.
- *Energy efficiency in manufacturing:* The manufacturing process of batteries is energy intensive. So intensive, that manufacturers of EV batteries benefit from the Energy Intensive Industry

compensation scheme which is a UK government initiative intended to help energy-intensive industries stay competitive as the economy transitions to zero carbon. The scheme provides relief for the costs of the UK Emissions Trading Scheme (ETS) and Carbon Price Support mechanism in their electricity bills, recognising that UK industrial electricity prices are higher than those of other countries. Consumption of such high volumes of power in the manufacturing process means there is a growing focus on ensuring such power is generated by renewable sources. Efforts are also underway to improve the energy efficiency of the manufacturing process.

It is important to remember that the EV industry is evolving rapidly, with ongoing efforts to enhance the sustainability of battery technologies.

5.3 Battery lifecycles

In many ways EVs are supplied with longer manufacturer warranties than ICEs; this is because the average EV battery is expected to have a 15-to-20-year life expectancy in a vehicle. Whereas ICEs usually carry warranties in the region of three years and 60,000 miles, battery cells from manufacturers such as Audi, BMW and Jaguar are warrantied for eight years and 100,000 miles. Tesla even goes as far as to warrant 150,000 miles on certain models (namely the Model S and Model X, though this is a reduction from their previously unlimited mileage battery warranty). To be able to call on most manufacturer's battery warranties a customer must see more than a 30% reduction of the battery capacity before the end of the warranty period.

Where battery performance falls below this 70% threshold manufacturers have recycling programmes for EV batteries. These enable the manufacturer to recover valuable materials and reduce the environmental impact of disposal. Nickel and cobalt, in particular, have a high enough value to justify the challenge and cost of recycling an EV battery.

Additionally, repurposing used batteries for stationary energy storage or other applications can extend their lifespan and reduce waste. Innovations in battery chemistry, recycling technologies and circular economy practices aim to address environmental concerns associated with EV batteries. We look at specific manufacturer shifts to try and combat the impact of battery creation later in this chapter at section 6.2 but examples of reutilising EV batteries include Nissan's use of retired car batteries to provide back-up power at Amsterdam Arena and Toyota's plan to power convenience stores in Japan via car batteries which are recharged via solar panels.

5.4 Lack of charging infrastructure and range anxiety

In the UK, the Department for Transport's (DfT) EV charging device statistics for January 2023 reveal that there were 37,055 public electric charging devices in the UK. Of these, 19% were 'rapid' devices (>25kW) and 57% were 'fast' chargers (7kW to 22kW). Around 49% of the devices were designated as 'destination' chargers, while 32% were 'on-street' chargers. Since January 2022, the number of public charging devices has increased by 31%.[10]

There is an uneven geographical distribution of charging devices, with London and Scotland having the highest provision per 100,000 population, and Northern Ireland, the Northwest, and Yorkshire and the Humber having the lowest provision. All regions in the UK saw an increase in total charging devices between October and December 2022, with Wales experiencing the greatest increase at 17.3%.[11]

The UK government recognises the importance of a comprehensive and reliable EV charging network. Measures have been taken to ensure sufficient charge points are installed in the coming years. Public charging infrastructure plays a crucial role in meeting the needs of existing and future EV owners for longer journeys and addressing the range concerns of potential future owners, thereby increasing EV uptake. The current public charging provision in the UK is comparable, if not favourable, to that of countries with more developed EV markets. Recently adopted provisions include the Public Charge Point Regulations 2023[12] which place various obligations on operators in respect of the operation and reporting of public charge points. Many of these obligations seem designed to empower customers: charge points must facilitate contactless payment, display the price in p/kWh and be 99% reliable across the operator's network – all these measures are likely to drive greater confidence in charging and protect consumers by offering better, more reliable services wherever they charge.

5.5 Grid capacity

Cornwall Insight predicts a significant increase in electricity demand due to the growing adoption of EVs. It has published a report[13] which estimates that by 2040, EVs will increase electricity demand by 71.6 TWh (terawatt-hours) annually in the UK. This surge in demand is attributed to the need for charging EV batteries.

As EV adoption increases, there is a need to ensure the electricity grid can accommodate the additional demand for charging, which involves the following:

- *Grid capacity and flexibility:* There is a need for investment in grid infrastructure to handle the increased load from EV charging. Additionally, there is potential for EVs to provide flexibility to the grid through smart charging and vehicle-to-grid (V2G) technologies, as seen in the public transport sector that is explored in section 3.1 of this chapter. These technologies allow EVs to act as energy storage devices, providing power back to the grid during peak demand periods, thus helping to balance supply and demand.

- *Charging infrastructure and integration:* There is a need for a widespread and accessible charging network, including both public and residential charging points. Integrating this network with renewable electricity sources can help reduce the carbon footprint associated with EV charging and support the transition to a greener energy system.
- *Collaboration and planning:* There needs to be collaboration between stakeholders – including energy providers, energy network operators, charging infrastructure operators and policymakers – to ensure a smooth transition to widespread EV adoption. Coordinated planning is required to identify areas of grid reinforcement, determine optimal charging locations and develop strategies for managing peak demand.

While the increase in electricity demand presents challenges, the flexibility of EV charging could be leveraged to support grid balancing and integrate renewable energy sources. Smart charging and vehicle-to-grid (V2G) technologies can enable EVs to provide services to the grid, such as load shifting and energy storage, contributing to a more sustainable and efficient energy system.

5.6 Cost of EVs vs ICE vehicles

One key barrier to widespread EV adoption is the fact that the upfront cost of EVs remains higher than traditional vehicles. As with many things, the cost of transitioning from an ICE to an EV is an important consideration for consumers in making the switch. Key considerations when buying an EV over an ICE include:

- *Purchase price:* In general, the initial purchase price of EVs tends to be higher than that of equivalent ICEs. In the UK, EV car purchasers could previously benefit from the plug-in vehicle grant but as discussed above this has been discontinued as the UK government focused its incentives elsewhere – and this shift is something that has been seen in other countries in Europe such as Germany. It should be noted that the difference in cost has been decreasing over the years as technology has advanced and manufacturers begin to benefit from economies of scale.
- *Running costs:* The cost of running an EV is (usually) cheaper overall than an ICE. This is because electricity is historically cheaper than fossil fuels on a per-mile basis and maintenance

costs for EVs are often lower due to their design having fewer moving parts. Currently EVs benefit from zero-rated road tax in the UK, however this policy is expected to end in April 2025.

- *Potential resale value:* Consumers often consider whether a vehicle will have a resale value when they are ready to change vehicles. It is difficult to predict the market for second hand EVs in the future – there is a case to be made that as battery technology (in particular) improves and becomes cheaper, this could have a negative impact on the value of older EVs.

The above factors are then taken together to give the total cost of ownership, which over the lifetime of a vehicle often mean that EVs become more cost-effective over their lifespan.

Financial incentives and increased manufacturing volumes can help reduce these costs over time. Interestingly the cost of a passenger battery EV has been reaching parity with that of its combustion engine equivalent. However, new rules of origin introduced in the EU in January 2024 (the rules stipulating a proportion of a vehicle must be made within the EU) has had the unintended consequence of increasing the price of EVs. While having the best of intentions (encouraging the development of a battery industry in the EU) the

One key barrier to widespread EV adoption is the fact that the upfront cost of EVs remains higher than traditional vehicles.

It is important to bear in mind that the EV market is dynamic, there are constant advancements, changing government incentives and new manufacturers entering the market, all of which will impact the cost of EVs.

new rules of origin may inadvertently reduce demand for EVs by increasing their initial purchase cost, because the EU battery manufacturing market is nowhere near as developed as its needs to be to avoid car manufacturers using batteries from the likes of China. Thus, these cars will attract a trade tariff which will only be passed on to the consumer in the form of a more expensive vehicle.

It is important to bear in mind that the EV market is dynamic, there are constant advancements, changing government incentives and new manufacturers entering the market, all of which will impact the cost of EVs.

6. How is the market responding to the challenges?

6.1 Collaborations

Governments, manufacturers and energy providers must work together to develop comprehensive strategies that prioritise ZEVs. This includes investing in research and development, building a robust and visible charging infrastructure and ensuring a sustainable supply chain for ZEVs.

Car manufacturers can collaborate to commoditise the manufacture of ZEVs. This is being seen already in the passenger EV market where

VW has strategic alliance with Ford to supply them with the parts to assemble the platform of an electric car. Similar arrangements have been announced between the likes of EV manufacturer, Lucid and Aston Martin as well as Lotus and Renault. These kinds of collaborations help achieve economies of scale with the purpose of driving down costs of development and manufacture, to make cars more affordable and develop and share new technologies across brands to make them more appealing to consumers.

Public authorities and private landlords can collaborate with charge point operators to establish visible and robust public charging networks that give the consumer the confidence that recharging an electric car is not going to be more of an inconvenience than refuelling at the pumps.

In terms of hydrogen – this fuel is most likely to be used first in buses. As such, public bodies who procure public transport solutions could be partnering with operators of buses, who are also in partnerships with hydrogen producers and hydrogen bus manufacturers – creating the full end to end hydrogen economy from demand to supply. This sector needs the certainty of demand being granted by a transport authority to justify the investment in production infrastructure.

6.2 Greening the manufacturing process

As well as the vehicles themselves, manufacturers are looking to reduce the emissions involved in their manufacturing processes. This is for a number of reasons. Firstly, companies are coming under pressure from shareholders and customers to demonstrate their environmental, social and governance (ESG) credentials. Secondly, a global rise in energy prices has led to more focus on ways to lower energy bills through reduced energy consumption. Further, installing renewable energy facilities at manufacturing plants can also be a way of reducing carbon footprint and costs at the same time while improving energy security as the OEM is in charge of the power generated.

An example of that is the Bentley car factory in Crewe, England which boasts the largest solar car park installed in the UK to date. It consists of 31,500 solar panels, now being increased to 36,416, which will cover an area of 60,911m^2, equivalent to nine football pitches or 311 tennis courts. That system supplements a previously installed rooftop solar array which together will be capable of delivering up to 75% of the plant's daytime electrical demand on average at a price lower than that they would otherwise pay taking power direct from the electricity grid. The Bentley project demonstrates how making the most of available rooftop and other land to install solar, batteries, wind or other renewable technology can reduce carbon footprint, energy costs and also provide a more robust, secure electricity supply for critical manufacturing processes.

The production of EVs presently results in higher emissions than the production of conventional ICE vehicles. This is mainly due to the process of manufacturing the battery itself which has been discussed at section 2.1 above. Locating the battery production facility in Europe, where electricity has a lower carbon intensity than, say, Asia, can help bring the production emissions down. The EU's Carbon Border Adjustment Mechanism (CBAM)[14] helps to offset the higher costs of battery production in Europe as imported batteries would have to pay a carbon tax. Similarly, the US's Inflation Reduction Act subsidises local battery production and promotes use of local components used to make the batteries: requiring a certain percentage of minerals from the US or countries with whom the US has a free trade agreement.

The good news is that, even with higher production emissions, EVs have lower lifetime emissions than ICE vehicles. EVs have zero emissions at the tailpipe and are powered by increasingly green electricity as the power grid decarbonises. When an EV battery reaches its end of life as a car battery, it can usually be reused either in homes as a battery storage system or on a wider scale to power a manufacturing plant or in a large-scale battery storage system.

In the UK, Japanese car manufacturer Nissan's EV36Zero project aims to make its Sunderland car manufacturing plant carbon neutral. It comprises the manufacture of ZEVs, renewable energy and on-site battery production. EV battery manufacturer, AESC, is building a huge 'gigafactory' next to the Nissan plant. Both Nissan and AESC will power their manufacturing processes with renewable energy generated on or near the plant.

Following suit, TATA Group (an Indian conglomerate) is also building a £4 billion EV car battery gigafactory in Somerset, England to supply primarily Jaguar Land Rover. The site was chosen over one in Spain and part of that decision was influenced by a reported £500 million in UK government incentives. Agrata, Tata's battery business, has said: "The 40GWh factory is set to be the biggest battery factory in the country and by the early 2030s will contribute almost half of the projected battery manufacturing capacity required for the UK automotive sector."[15] It is anticipated that production lines will be operational by 2026.

6.3 Developing the charging infrastructure

To drive the adoption of EVs, governments and policymakers must continue to implement measures such as subsidies, tax breaks and stricter emission standards. Adopting more stringent regulations on

Adopting more stringent regulations on vehicle emissions will further cultivate a favourable environment for the growth of the EV market.

vehicle emissions will further cultivate a favourable environment for the growth of the EV market. For example, in West Yorkshire where, following the announcement of the new Clean Air Zones to be adopted in Leeds and Bradford, the West Yorkshire Combined Authority invested £1.2 million into the installation of 88 EV charge points that could be used for taxis and private vehicles.[16] Similar initiatives are being seen in cities and towns across the UK such as Glasgow, Manchester and London.

These incentives encourage consumers to choose EVs over traditional vehicles, reducing greenhouse gas (GHG) emissions. Government bodies are instrumental in driving the development of EV charging infrastructure through policies, incentives and regulations. They provide guidance on charging infrastructure deployment, funding opportunities and planning requirements.

Governments are also investing in public charging infrastructure to create a reliable and accessible charging network. For instance, the UK government has established the Office for Zero Emission Vehicles (OZEV) to support the expansion of EV charging infrastructure. Governments worldwide – including the US, India, parts of Asia (Japan, South Korea and Malaysia among others) and across much of Europe – are taking steps to ensure the availability of charging infrastructure to meet the growing demand for EVs.

Industry bodies and associations are actively involved in shaping the future of EV charging infrastructure. They provide guidance, standards and best practices to ensure interoperability, safety and efficiency in charging systems. For example, the International Electrotechnical Commission (IEC) and the Society of Automotive Engineers (SAE) have developed standards for EV charging connectors and communication protocols. Additionally, organisations like the Charging Interface Initiative (CharIN)[17] are working towards establishing global standards for high-power charging. These industry bodies and associations play a vital role in harmonising charging infrastructure and promoting a seamless charging experience for EV owners.

This is alongside regulation such as the Public Charge Point Regulations 2023 in the UK which specify a reliability standard for rapid charge points and the Alternative Fuels Infrastructure Regulation[18] which came into force on 13 April 2024 in the EU which sets minimum targets for publicly accessible charge points. Both the UK and EU regulations also specify that charge points must have transparent pricing and offer payment via a credit or debit card.

Leading OEMs and EV companies play a crucial role in driving the development of EV charging infrastructure. As well as investing in

Expanding charging infrastructure is crucial to support the widespread adoption of EVs. Collaborative efforts between governments, private companies and utilities are needed to invest in the development of charging networks.

research and development to improve charging technologies, increase battery range and enhance the overall EV ownership experience, these companies are also collaborating with charging infrastructure providers to establish reliable and convenient charging networks. By offering innovative charging solutions and expanding their charging networks, OEMs and EV companies are facilitating the widespread adoption of EVs. One of the most notable of charging networks that has been developed by an automaker is the Tesla Supercharger network – a global network of rapid charging stations which is integrated into the software of each Tesla vehicle, thus simplifying the charging and payment process. Until May 2022, the Tesla supercharger network was exclusive for Tesla drivers, however since then a small number of sites on the network have allowed for third party compatible EV charging. At the same time, Ionity – a joint venture between major OEMs including BMW Group, Ford Motor Company, Hyundai Motor Group, Mercedes Benz and Volkswagen Group – aims to boost confidence in the EV sector throughout Europe by building its network of fast chargers open to all vehicle types across 24 European countries.

Expanding charging infrastructure is crucial to support the widespread adoption of EVs. Collaborative efforts between governments, private companies and utilities are needed to invest in the development of charging networks. This includes the establishment of fast-charging stations along highways, workplace charging solutions and residential charging infrastructure. By providing convenient and accessible charging options, range anxiety can be alleviated, making EV ownership more feasible and attractive for consumers.

Integrating EVs into the broader energy system is another critical aspect of achieving sustainable transport. Smart grid technologies can optimise charging patterns, manage energy demand and integrate renewable energy sources. By coordinating EV charging with renewable energy generation, the reliance on fossil fuels can be reduced, maximising the environmental benefits of EVs. Public-private collaboration plays a crucial role in driving innovation, accelerating the deployment of charging infrastructure and creating a favourable environment for EV adoption. Governments should provide supportive policies and regulations, while private companies invest in research, infrastructure deployment and innovative business models.

6.4 Government regulation and funding

Achieving the required level of charging infrastructure to support the rapid growth of EV sales is not always possible without help from government. This is certainly the case in the UK. Ideally, the government prefers to leave the growth of charging infrastructure to market forces but using powers under the Automated and Electric

Vehicles Act 2018 it is able to step in where necessary (eg, where there has been a market failure, most commonly a lack of charging infrastructure in rural locations or where connection costs to the local grid network are too high).

In March 2022, the UK government published the Electric Vehicle Infrastructure Strategy,[19] setting out its strategic approach to delivering infrastructure that is required for it to meet its net zero targets. It has said that its vision for 2030 is to remove charging infrastructure as a perceived and real barrier to adoption of EVs and where EV charging will be cheaper and more convenient than refuelling at a petrol station. It expects there to be 300,000 public charge points as a minimum in the UK. Its main goals are:

- everyone to be able to find and access reliable public charge points wherever they live;
- effortless on- and off-street charging for private and commercial drivers;
- fairly priced and inclusively designed public charging;
- market-led rollout for the majority of charge points with limited intervention only to address market failures;
- infrastructure seamlessly integrated into a smart energy system; and
- continued innovation to meet drivers' needs.

Some of these goals have been addressed in the recent Public Charge Point Regulations 2023, which were made using powers under the Automated and Electric Vehicles Act 2018. The Public Charge Point Regulations 2023 place obligations on owners or operators of public charge points including to allow contactless payment methods, display the price in pence per kilowatt hour, maintain a 99% reliability standard and provide various data.

(a) On-street charging

The development of infrastructure is not just limited to public charge points at strategic, well-travelled locations. A notable hurdle to the increased adoption of EVs is a lack of drivers having access to private charge points that enable them to charge their EVs at their home. This is somewhat mitigated in the new-build residential sector by recent amendments to the Building Regulations 2010[20] which require the instalment of electric charge points in new residential buildings.

However, those without off-street parking still face major challenges if they want to charge anywhere other than 'on-the-go'. The UK government's On-Street Residential Charge Point Scheme[21] provides local authorities with funding to help with the cost of on-street charging points in residential areas. This scheme is designed to support the installation of charge points in areas where off-street parking is not widely available and covers up to 75% of the capital costs of installing such charge points.

(b) Rapid Charging Fund (RCF)

The RCF provides financial support to local authorities, private companies and other organisations to install rapid charging infrastructure at key locations across the country. The fund aims to address the current gaps in the rapid charging network and ensure that EV drivers have access to convenient and reliable charging options, particularly for long-distance travel.

The fund supports the installation of high-powered ultra-rapid chargers, typically with a charging capacity of 150kW or higher. These chargers can significantly reduce charging times compared to standard chargers, allowing EV drivers to quickly top up their vehicles' batteries during longer journeys.

The RCF will fund grid connections for ultra-rapid chargers where they would otherwise be prohibitively expensive. It will allow chargers to be installed at locations on motorways and strategic A-roads that are most convenient for drivers, rather than be restricted to where there

A notable hurdle to the increased adoption of EVs is a lack of drivers having access to private charge points that enable them to charge their EVs at their home.

is sufficient power on the grid. The grid connections will be future-proofed, allowing for connections to be sized to meet forecast demand levels which reflect the expected growth in demand for EV charging as EV adoption increases and sales of petrol and diesel vehicles are phased-out.

(c) Local Electric Vehicle Infrastructure (LEVI) Fund

The LEVI refers to a government funding initiative in the UK that aims to support the development and expansion of EV charging infrastructure at the local level. The LEVI fund provides financial assistance to local authorities and other organisations to install EV charging points in their respective areas.

The LEVI fund is intended to help local communities and regions improve their EV charging infrastructure, making it more accessible and convenient for EV owners. By increasing the availability of charging points in local areas, the programme aims to encourage the adoption of EVs and facilitate longer journeys from and to those local communities.

The funding provided through the LEVI fund can be used to install various types of EV charging infrastructure, including rapid chargers, fast chargers and destination chargers. The specific charging solutions implemented under the programme depend on the needs and priorities of each local authority or organisation.

The LEVI fund is part of the UK government's broader efforts to create a comprehensive and accessible EV charging network across the country. By supporting local authorities in expanding their charging infrastructure, the programme contributes to the overall goal of transitioning to a greener and more sustainable transportation system.

(d) Renewable Transport Fuel Obligation (RTFO)

The RTFO is a scheme that supports the uptake of renewable fuels in vehicles, so applies to hydrogen-powered vehicles and those powered by other sustainable fuels such as biofuels. It is an obligation on suppliers of liquid fossil fuel for use in transport in the UK. A proportion of the overall fuel they supply must come from sustainable fuel. This proportion increases each year up to 2032, when the scheme is currently due to end.

Suppliers fulfil this obligation by buying and redeeming Renewable Transport Fuel Certificates (RTFCs) which are issued to renewable transport fuels. Normally these tend to be bioethanol or biodiesel which is produced from food or non-food crops. But hydrogen and renewable fuels of non-biological origin (RFNBOs) are also eligible for RTFCs[22] and the government is expanding the scheme to include recycled carbon fuels produced from fossil fuel wastes that cannot be avoided, reused or recycled,[23] which will particularly benefit sustainable aviation fuels (see further Chapter VII).

Since its introduction in 2008 the RTFO has helped to lower the UK's transport emissions. In 2022, renewable fuel made up 6.8% of total transport fuel, with an average GHG saving of 82% when compared to fossil fuel use.[24]

7. Conclusion: why could zero emission vehicles be helpful to reaching net zero target?

Zero emission vehicles play a pivotal role in the global pursuit of achieving a net zero carbon future. The transportation sector is a major contributor to GHG emissions across the globe, with road vehicles being a significant source. According to data from the UK's National Atmospheric Emissions Inventory (NAEI), road transport accounted for approximately 21% of the total GHG emissions in the UK in 2019.[25] Transitioning to zero emission or electric vehicles is crucial for reducing these emissions.

By relying on electricity as a power source, these vehicles eliminate tailpipe emissions, mitigating air pollution and decreasing reliance on fossil fuels. The transition to renewable energy generation and the resultant decarbonisation of electricity grids, this strengthens the case for EVs, making them an integral part of the move to reduce overall carbon emissions in the transportation sector. As for other technologies, they will also play their part. With the utilisation of green and sustainable fuels such as hydrogen and biofuels where electricity does not provide the best solution (eg, HGVs).

Uptake is expected to increase considerably over the next few years as mandates take effect and countries adopt ICE phase-out targets. Battery and other technologies will continue to improve which should bring down both costs and carbon emissions in manufacturing. Grids need to keep up so there needs to be collaboration between the energy and transport industries and those responsible for planning the charging infrastructure.

Notes

1 IEA, Global EV Outlook 2023, "Trends in batteries", www.iea.org/reports/global-ev-outlook-2023/trends-in-batteries.
2 IEA, Global EV Outlook 2023, "Trends in charging infrastructure", www.iea.org/reports/global-ev-outlook-2023/trends-in-charging-infrastructure.
3 HM Government, "The Ten Point Plan for a Green Industrial Revolution", November 2020, https://assets.publishing.service.gov.uk/media/5fb5513de90e0720978b1a6f/10_POINT_PLAN_BOOKLET.pdf.
4 Department for Transport (DfT), "A zero emission vehicle (ZEV) mandate and CO2 emissions regulation for new cars and vans in the UK", 30 March 2023, www.gov.uk/government/consultations/a-zero-emission-vehicle-zev-mandate-and-co2-emissions-regulation-for-new-cars-and-vans-in-the-uk.
5 SI 2023 No 1394.

6 Regulation (EU) 2019/631 (as amended by Regulation (EU) 2023/851).
7 See Accelerating to Zero Coalition, "Zero Emission Vehicles Declaration", https://acceleratingtozero.org/the-declaration/.
8 BloombergNEF, "Zero-Emission Vehicles Factbook: A BloombergNEF special report prepared for COP27", November 2022, https://assets.bbhub.io/professional/sites/24/2022-COP27-ZEV-Transition_Factbook.pdf.
9 McKinsey & Company, "The race to decarbonize electric-vehicle batteries", 23 February 2023, www.mckinsey.com/industries/automotive-and-assembly/our-insights/the-race-to-decarbonize-electric-vehicle-batteries.
10 DfT, "Electric vehicle charging device statistics: April 2023", www.gov.uk/government/statistics/electric-vehicle-charging-device-statistics-april-2023/electric-vehicle-charging-device-statistics-april-2023.
11 *Ibid*.
12 SI 2023 No 1168.
13 Cornwall Insight, "EVs are predicted to increase electricity demand by 71.6TWh", 15 September 2021, www.cornwall-insight.com/press/evs-are-predicted-to-increase-electricity-demand-by-71-6twh/.
14 See https://taxation-customs.ec.europa.eu/carbon-border-adjustment-mechanism_en#legislative-documents.
15 Robert Lea, "Tata to build 'gigafactory' in Somerset", *The Times*, 28 February 2024, www.thetimes.com/life-style/driving/article/27tata-jb89nqhck#:~:text=%E2%80%9CThe%2040GWh%20factory%20is%20set,will%20be%20its%20anchor%20customer.
16 Equans, "The West Yorkshire Combined Authority", www.equans.co.uk/sites/g/files/tkmtob116/files/2022-01/The%20West%20Yorkshire%20Combined%20Authority%20and%20EQUANS.pdf.
17 See www.charin.global/.
18 See https://eur-lex.europa.eu/legal-content/EN/TXT/?uri=CELEX%3A32023R1804.
19 HM Government, "Taking charge: the electric vehicle infrastructure strategy", https://assets.publishing.service.gov.uk/media/6245ba40e90e075f15381cf0/taking-charge-the-electric-vehicle-infrastructure-strategy.pdf.
20 SI 2010 No 2214.
21 Energy Saving Trust, "On-street residential chargepoint scheme", https://energysavingtrust.org.uk/grants-and-loans/on-street-residential-chargepoint-scheme/.
22 For more detail on hydrogen and the RTFO, see the Addleshaw Goddard briefing, "When can green and blue hydrogen get extra RTFO certificates?", 12 August 2022, www.addleshawgoddard.com/en/insights/insights-briefings/2022/energy/when-can-green-blue-hydroge-extra-rtfo-certificates/.
23 See Section 157 of the Energy Act 2023.
24 GOV.UK, "Renewable fuel statistics 2022: final report", 8 November 2023, www.gov.uk/government/statistics/renewable-fuel-statistics-2022-final-report/renewable-fuel-statistics-2022-final-report#long-term-trends.
25 Department for Business, Energy & Industrial Strategy, "2019 UK Greenhouse Gas Emissions, Final Figures", 2 February 2021, https://assets.publishing.service.gov.uk/media/60198cd5d3bf7f70bc2e1ee7/2019_Final_greenhouse_gas_emissions_statistical_release.pdf.

IV. Public transport and payments*

Jack Houselander
Euan Towers
Addleshaw Goddard

1. Introduction

How we pay for things plays a key role in driving uptake and use. Payments can shape consumer behaviour and business models and can determine how successful a particular business or service will be. Ease and convenience are paramount. Modern consumers expect quick, 'frictionless' payment experiences. Any hurdles or complexities in the payment process can deter them from using a product or service.

Innovations like digital wallets, contactless payments, wearable payment methods and one-click purchasing have revolutionised the payment landscape, making it significantly easier to pay for things, and helping to make certain services highly appealing to consumers.

Uber and Amazon are obvious paradigms, with their ultra-smooth payment and checkout experiences encouraging repeat business and fostering customer loyalty. But there are many more examples out there; the ubiquity of PayPal and Klarna as payment options; the ease of paying with Apple and GooglePay; and the rise of subscription, or 'card on file', based payments, being just a few.

*On 4 July 2024 there was a change in UK government which introduced some new policy impacting the topics covered in this chapter. As this chapter was drafted before these updates were announced in the King's Speech on 24 July, please refer to the Addendum on page 183 for insight on these emerging policy updates.

We now expect the same smooth payment experience we have with some organisations to be the same everywhere. Most people will feel a real sense of frustration when making a purchase is awkward and takes a lot of time.

This is true for all industries, but it's especially important in transportation. If it's easy and convenient to pay for public transport, more people will use it. To encourage people to pick public transport over driving alone, so that there is reduced traffic congestion and lower carbon emissions, public transport must be very easy to use. Failing to make public transport easy and convenient to pay for, by contrast, could have the opposite effect. Yes, there will always be a baseline minimum user-base for public transport options, that is, people who have no other alternative but to use them; but the path to decarbonisation requires operators to persuade car owners to leave their vehicle at home and to take the bus or train instead.

It is little wonder, therefore, that the UK government has made the streamlining of payment methods offered to drivers and transport users a central part of its "Better, Greener Britain" plans to decarbonise transport.[1]

1.1 Aims and overview

This chapter aims to:

- set out the legal and compliance context in relation to payment services;
- set out a basic payment transaction and the relevant parties involved in it;
- consider single payment environments in open loop and closed loop systems; and
- set out some of the key legal considerations that need to be thought about from the outset when designing and implementing the payments functionality of a single transport system.

2. Payment services: the legal and compliance context

In the United Kingdom, the payments landscape is regulated by a range of different legislation, Financial Conduct Authority (FCA) rules and guidance, and industry rules, such as those published by each major payment method ('payment network rules') which apply to the use of their particular payment methods. This creates a complex legal framework which can be challenging to navigate.

2.1 Financial regulation

The primary set of rules governing payments in the UK are the Payment Services Regulations 2017 (PSRs),[2] which implements the European Union's revised Payment Services Directive (PSD2)[3] into UK law.[4]

The PSRs define the legal framework for payment services, including card payments, account-to-account payments, open banking (including payment initiation services) and account information services, with electronic money services being regulated under the Electronic Money Regulations 2011[5] (EMRs). The PSRs and EMRs set out the foundations for the UK payments landscape and set out what a payment service is and which are regulated.

The PSRs and the EMRs are overlaid by regulations which apply depending on the type of payment and the product that is being offered. These include the Payment Account Regulations 2015,[6] the SEPA Regulations 2012,[7] the Cross-Border Payments Regulation 2019[8] and the Interchange Fee Regulation 2015.[9]

There are also regulations which apply to financial crime such as the Money Laundering Regulations 2017[10] which require firms to carry out due diligence on their customers and to put in place systems and controls to prevent financial crime. The Wire Transfer Regulations 2015[11] work alongside the Money Laundering Regulations and requires firms acting for a payer to transmit certain information with the payment (such as the address and name of the payer). The aim of this is to make payments systems more transparent and harder to abuse.

To encourage people to pick public transport over driving alone, so that there is reduced traffic congestion and lower carbon emissions, public transport must be very easy to use.

So, any organisation providing a payment service in the UK must consider whether they need to be authorised by the FCA or the Prudential Regulation Authority (PRA), and will also need a well-resourced compliance function in order to manage the range of compliance and conduct requirements that need to be satisfied in order to carry on payment services.

2.2 Payment network rules

Each payment method operates through a 'payment network'. A payment network is the entity which governs and provides the contractual, commercial, technical and operational framework within which a payment method can function and under which the participants in a payment network cooperate. A discussion of who usually participates in a payment network is set out in section 4.1 below.

Well-known payment networks include Visa, Mastercard, American Express and PayPal. Each payment network has its own set of rules which set out the roles and responsibilities of each of the participants in the payment network. These ultimately determine how payments can be accepted as a means of payment and how those payments are processed and settled.

One of the key concepts set out in most payment network rules is the 'buyer protection regime' which allows cardholders to reverse a transaction, and recover the transaction amount, in the event of a dispute.

One of the key concepts set out in most payment network rules is the 'buyer protection regime' which allows cardholders to reverse a transaction, and recover the transaction amount, in the event of a dispute. The scope of such buyer protection regimes varies between the payment networks (and payment methods) but the most well-known are the 'chargeback' regimes in the Visa and Mastercard payment network rules.

These regimes have no statutory or regulatory footing and are effected contractually through the payment network rules and the various contracts between those participating in the payment network. These are particularly relevant for merchants wishing to accept that payment method because the risk of a valid dispute is ultimately allocated to the merchant. An outline of how chargeback operates and discussion of this topic is set out in section 4 below.

2.3 Data protection

Data protection legislation plays a key role in safeguarding personal data privacy and security. This includes some of the payment data that is used for processing payments. The foundational data protection legislation in the UK is currently the Data Protection Act 2018 and the retained EU law version of the EU General Data Protection Regulation (Regulation (EU) 2016/679),[12] known as the UK GDPR.

Anyone involved in collecting, storing or otherwise processing payments data must comply with these principles, ensuring transparent data practices, informed consent and appropriate security measures when handling personal data. At the same time, parties will want to use the data captured and generated for their own purposes. For example, a transport network operator may wish to track payment methods used to monitor travel patterns and user behaviour and should do so in a manner that complies with data protection legislation.

In addition to data protection legislation, there are industry standards for data security which may apply depending on the payment method. The Payment Card Industry Data Security Standard (PCI DSS)[13] maintained by the PCI Security Standards Council is a common example of this which sets the framework for secure handling of payment card data. These standards (including the PCI DSS) are not legislation and are usually given force contractually through the payment network rules (see section 2.2 above).

Again, this only increases the complexity and compliance burden in being able to take payments, particularly when (as would be the case with any public transport operator) this is done at scale and means that any operator looking at how they can optimise their 'take payments' strategy will need expert advice.

Most organisations looking to make new payment methodologies available to their customers tend to rely on the services of specialised payment service providers rather than attempting to handle funds and payments entirely by themselves.

3. The payment service provider relationship

Partly as a result of the compliance challenges discussed in section 2 above, most organisations looking to make new payment methodologies available to their customers tend to rely on the services of specialised payment service providers rather than attempting to handle funds and payments entirely by themselves.

The need for cutting edge technology to be at the centre of any organisation's strategy for taking payments has also strengthened this trend. Selecting the right payment service provider to partner with, and negotiating a comprehensive service agreement with them, is therefore a key consideration for any transport authority/operator looking at modernising their ticketing and payment operations.

4. How does a payment transaction work?

4.1 Key actors

Before considering how a single payment environment could be structured in a transport context, it is helpful to set out how a basic payment transaction works and the key actors needed for this.

Key parties are likely to include the following:

- *The cardholder:* The customer (or passenger) who has a payment card.
- *The issuer:* Typically, the bank which holds the cardholder's bank account and issues them a card. The issuer will approve or decline transactions requests by checking, for example, that the cardholder has funds in their bank account and has properly authorised the payment transaction.
- *The merchant:* This is the transport operator who provides the transport service, decides on and publishes the applicable fares and ultimately receives payment of the relevant amount from the cardholder.
- *A technology partner:* Given the technical scale and complexity of implementing an open loop payment system for transport, the merchant will usually partner with a dedicated technology provider who will supply the contactless payment terminals and the relevant back-office systems, and help to manage the integration of the transport operators systems with those of the acquirer.
- *The acquirer:* This is the bank or payment service provider that processes and settles payment transactions for the merchant. The acquirer will be registered with a card scheme, and will work with the relevant technology provider to ensure they can receive payment transactions and data from the transport operators systems and then process that properly. Most large transport operators will likely operate with a number of different acquirers to optimise cost and ensure 24/7 availability of the service.
- *A payment network:* For example, Visa, Mastercard and Amex, who provide the network that connects acquirers and issuers, and facilitates the processing of each individual card payment, the communication of authorisation requests, the reconciliation and calculation of aggregate amounts to be settled between issuers and acquirers on a daily basis, and the resolution of any payment disputes.

4.2 Payment transaction process

The steps in a basic payment transaction can be described as follows. For simplicity, this assumes a card is used as the payment method although similar processes are followed by other mainstream payment networks.

- *Capture:* This is where the transaction and the cardholder's card data and data about the sale (eg, amount) are 'captured' by the payment terminal in relation to services (eg, an e-ticket for a train journey) the cardholder is purchasing from the merchant. These data are submitted by the payment terminal to the acquirer on behalf of the merchant for authorisation.

- *Authorisation:* These 'captured' data are then submitted by the acquirer to the card issuer (via the card scheme) for fraud checking and to check there are sufficient funds available in the cardholder's account for the transaction. If authorised, the card issuer will block those funds in the cardholder's account pending settlement.
- *Processing:* If the transaction is authorised, then at this point the merchant enables the cardholder to utilise the services (eg, by issuing an e-ticket for a train journey) and the cardholder continues with their journey. At certain points during the day, the merchant sends details of all its authorised transactions to its acquirer for settlement.
- *Settlement:* The acquirer collects the funds for those authorised transactions from the relevant card issuers (through a process managed by the card schemes) and pays them out to the merchant. Settlement usually occurs on the next business day but can take longer depending on the acquirer and transaction type.

4.3 Chargebacks

'Chargeback' is a form of buyer protection operated by the major card schemes. It allows a cardholder to reverse a transaction and recover the transaction amount in circumstances where the cardholder did not receive the services promised from the merchant, or if a transaction was made fraudulently or in error by the merchant.

The cardholder can raise a dispute with their card issuer which, if valid, would be paid for by the merchant's acquirer. The acquirer would then need to recoup this amount from the merchant. This is normally done pursuant to the merchant services agreement the acquirer has in place with the merchant.

In a transport network context, chargeback risk can present in various ways:

- First, it is not always possible for the acquirer to request authorisation from the card issuer in real time for certain transactions (eg, if there is no connectivity on a ferry/bus or in an underground station), but this usually does not prevent the cardholder from travelling (eg, where the need to get the passengers through the turnstiles outweighs the benefit of waiting for an authorisation 'confirmed' response from the card issuing bank). This presents a risk that a cardholder could raise a chargeback claim on the basis the transaction was not authorised which could be ultimately passed back to the transport provider (as the merchant).
- Similarly, it may simply be that a cardholder does not actually

Understanding these chargeback liability risks, and working with payment services providers to put in place appropriate mitigants, will be an important consideration for any operator looking to replace tickets with payment cards.

have enough funds in their bank account for the ticket they are 'tapping' their card to buy. In this case, while the cardholder themselves should not seek a chargeback, a card issuer who did not have an opportunity to send back an 'authorisation declined' response due to the lack of funds in the cardholder's bank account can nonetheless decline the transaction or raise a chargeback.

- Another possibility is that a cardholder might argue that they were not aware of the ticket fare or the final journey cost when they tapped their card to travel or might contact their bank to say they 'forgot to tap out' and have been charged the wrong amount.

Understanding these chargeback liability risks, and working with payment services providers to put in place appropriate mitigants, will be an important consideration for any operator looking to replace tickets with payment cards.

In the UK, the card payment and transit industries have developed a risk sharing framework aimed at enabling the use of credit and debit cards for contactless travel.[14] For example, the card issuing industry has agreed to share the risk of chargebacks with Transport for London (TfL) in the context of the London Underground contactless credit/debit card ticketing system, despite TfL's use of 'offline authorisations'. This risk sharing framework applies instead of the standard payment network rules position that this risk would sit entirely with the merchant, which might otherwise have dissuaded TfL from launching its new system.

Use cases and practical deployments (and the associated chargeback risks) may, of course, vary between different transport operators and modes of transport. For example, it is unlikely that contactless payments will be used in all instances and for all types of tickets. But it is noteworthy that, for a large-scale deployment at least, a pragmatic solution was found.

5. 'Open loop' and 'closed loop' payments in transport

Having simple and ubiquitous ways of paying for a variety of transport options within a transport network in a consistent and consolidated way can help drive uptake of those transport options by customers. In this section, we consider 'open loop' and 'closed loop' payment systems which can support using single payment methods across a transport network.

Payment methods can be either 'open loop' or 'closed loop'. Open loop is the name given to a payment method that can be used anywhere

Having simple and ubiquitous ways of paying for a variety of transport options within a transport network in a consistent and consolidated way can help drive uptake of those transport options by customers.

which accepts that payment method – for example, most Visa or Mastercard branded payment cards. Closed loop means a payment method only works in specific places or for specific uses – for example, store gift cards.

In the transit sector, open loop payments generally refer to the use of bank-issued contactless credit and debit cards (eg, Visa, Mastercard or Amex) instead of closed loop transit authority/operator alternatives, such as the Oyster Card in London.

For public transport, open loop payments are then often combined with eliminating any standalone ticketing system – so that the payment credential (ie, typically the credit or debit card) also takes the place of any separate physical/paper ticket.

Open loop systems typically rely on the use of contactless payment devices, which are equipped with 'near field communication' technology. Passengers simply need to tap their contactless payment device on a card reader located at the entrance or exit of transportation modes, such as buses, trains, or subway stations. The reader then communicates with the payment network to verify and authorise the payment transaction. These contactless payment devices are usually linked to a payment card, but this does not have to be the case and they may also be linked to another payment method such as a digital wallet. The payment network then securely processes the transaction, deducting the amount of the fare from the passenger's account. The system also records the transaction data, which can be used by the transit authority/operator for fare reconciliation and ridership analysis.

5.1 Pros of open loop

The benefits of open loop systems for transport are generally obvious.

(a) Benefits for consumers in simplicity and ease of use

If anyone asked Londoners whether they would wish to go back to the old, closed loop Oyster or paper ticketed system compared with the current 'tap in, tap out' payment card-based system, the answer would be almost unanimous in favour of open loop.

For visitors to London, travelling around town has also become a far easier experience, without the need to learn how the Oyster or paper ticket system works, and knowing that the system will simply take the right fare from their card rather than having to spend significant time trying to figure out the right ticket to request from the machine or worry about residual value being left on the card at the end of their trip.

As well as the enhanced user experience, there are also significant practical efficiencies.

(b) Legacy, closed loop systems are expensive to operate
Transport for London has suggested that as much as 14p in every £1 collected was spent on maintaining and operating the Oyster payment system. By contrast, open loop can be operated for as little as 10p of every £1 spent. This may sound like a small amount, but when you scale it up over total revenues that are in the billions, the annual cost savings for TfL in switching to an open loop system from the closed loop Oyster card are likely to have been over £100 million.

(c) There is also some environmental benefit in eliminating separate tickets
Physical tickets require paper or cardboard, and closed loop payment cards (such as Oyster) are usually cut from plastic. It is far better from the environment to just use a payment card the user is already carrying rather than anything new.

(d) Safety and convenience
From a safety and convenience perspective, customers queuing to reload prepaid fare media or obtain paper tickets at busy times is largely eliminated by open loop systems.

Transport operators can reduce or eliminate the need for ticketing and vending machines, saving money on capital and maintenance costs. This allows transport operators to focus far more on their core business – operating and optimising the transport network; and removes the administrative burden and cost of running a complex ticketing system alongside that.

5.2 Cons of open loop
Of course, while there is a range of highly compelling arguments in favour of open loop, making its adoption by transport networks almost a 'no brainer', there are some downsides that need to be taken into account.

Implementation complexity and cost is a key issue and probably explains why open loop payment and ticketing systems remain relatively rare in the transport sector at the time of writing.

(a) Cost implications
The cost of implementing an open loop system on public transport will almost certainly require government funding, and large travelling populations to justify them; not all countries/cities will be able to afford the cost.

(b) Lack of access to electronic payment methods

There also remain many people who need to use public transport who either do not have access to a credit or debit card, or simply prefer to use cash or legacy ticketing systems with which they are familiar. Some people object to using bank issued credit/debit card at all due to the data processing that is involved and the privacy concerns they have about this creating a record of their spending; they would prefer to remain anonymous.

(c) Continued need to maintain residual own credential or paper-based capability

Any public transport operator that implements open loop is unlikely to be able to move wholesale to that system, and will probably need to maintain some residual own credential or paper based capability. Most operators will therefore wish to find a way to integrate this into a single turnstile or payment point, which can accept bank issued credit or debit cards, or the operator's own proprietary method (such as Oyster) or paper-based tickets. This is all doable, but bespoke hardware of this nature only increases the cost and complexity of implementation.

(d) Risk of rider-fraud and/or chargebacks

As noted above, the risk of rider-fraud and/or chargebacks is also something that needs to be carefully considered and managed. If a transport operator currently operates a system requiring a user to purchase a ticket before boarding, then they have been paid for each journey before it even begins. Open loop systems don't necessarily work that way, however – with riders sometimes required to tap in and tap out themselves and to do so honestly at the start and end of their journey.

Some turnstiles (such as those in big cities) need to let passengers in so quickly that there isn't even time (around three seconds) to complete a full online connection with the cardholder's bank to confirm that there are funds in the account and that the consumer's bank account is still operational.

This is not to say that there are no fraud risks in other systems, but there are unique risks with open loop systems that will need to be designed for at the outset and constantly managed through the operation of the system. For example, some transport operators will force an online authorisation to be sought, even if that creates some delay at the turnstile, where a particular payment card has not been used on the system for a pre-defined period, or if the cumulative value of chargeable fares exceeds a threshold.

(e) Transparency and customer understanding concerns
Finally, there can also be transparency and customer understanding concerns where it becomes so easy to pay that you almost don't necessarily even notice or realise that you are doing it or how much you are spending. How many Londoners in 2024 know how much they actually pay for a bus journey or a tube ride when they take it? Are we, as is required under regulation,[15] truly consenting to the payment transaction we're making when we tap in and tap out?

There is a level of trust involved that the transport operator's system is going to work perfectly and deduct the right fare, but even where it does this, could some riders argue that they haven't really been made aware of the price? This is an issue which would perhaps be more acute for higher value journeys, or network operators who have a very wide list of different fares, than those with lower value or less variable ticket prices.

There may also be some practical/operational issues that need to be carefully managed to avoid problems – for example, what if a cardholder has multiple credit/debit cards and taps in with one, and out with another? Or what if they accidentally tap two cards at once?

How many Londoners in 2024 know how much they actually pay for a bus journey or a tube ride when they take it? Are we, as is required under regulation, truly consenting to the payment transaction we're making when we tap in and tap out?

It is likely that the transport network operator will bear some operational cost of dealing with a small minority of passengers who raise payment-related disputes and queries with them; a cost which is no doubt offset by the cost savings elsewhere, but it is something that will need to be designed for and managed by any similar transport operator serious about implementing open loop.

6. Models

Any operator of an open loop payment and ticketing system in the transport space will also need to consider what fare and payment model they need and wish to operate. Examples include the following:

- *Single, pay-as-you-go:* In this model, the fare is known beforehand – it is either a flat fare, or inputted into the device by the driver or customer before the takes place. Card payment could be either contactless or require PIN entry. This model may work well for single-use fixed-fare journeys – such as in city bus journeys.
- *Aggregated pay-as-you-go:* The fare is calculated at the end of a defined period (eg, a day) or after a completed chargeable fare by processing all the taps and calculating the appropriate fare. Caps may be applied so that the fare can never go above a certain daily or weekly level. This model may work well for public transport where users may take multiple journeys but with an aggregated area – again, this model could be applied to in city bus journeys.
- *Pre-purchase:* For higher value fares, a transport operator may prefer to require the cardholder to pre-purchase their ticket, in advance of travel, and then the payment card used to buy the ticket would be used as a ticket/proof of purchase, but without payment needing to be taken at the point of boarding the transport. This option might work well for longer distance journeys, and especially for pre-purchased 'return' tickets, rather than 'in city' travel.
- *Variable fares – pre-authorisation:* In this model, the fare is not known beforehand, because it will depend, for example, on where the traveller disembarks and ends their journey. The payment will be processed as a pre-authorisation, which confirms the validity of the card, and may place a hold for a certain amount of funds from the cardholder's account pending the final transaction amount being known. This model may work well for public transport where users may take multiple journeys but with variable costs per journey (eg, this is the model used on the London Underground).
- *Recurring payments:* Another model could involve the transport user giving consent for the transport operator to periodically collect payments from an agreed payment method according to

the fares incurred by the transport user. These payments might be collected using payment card details stored on file, by direct debit collection, or using new payment methods which are coming to market such as a variable recurring payment under which the transport user would allow a transport operator to collect varying fare amounts from its bank account. This model could work well for transport operators with a separate app used for booking journeys (eg, Uber and Bolt use this model).

The point of the above examples is not to exhaustively detail all the different models and payment options that could be used by different transport operators. Rather, we have set this out to note that there are a number of quite different models available, and a range of different payment network and other rules and considerations which will apply to each.

For example, the use of payment card data for any purpose other than making a payment is strictly controlled under payment network rules, so in the pre-purchase model, the subsequent use of a payment card simply as a 'ticket' or proof of purchase to permit entry into the vehicle would need to be carefully worked through to ensure this is done in a compliant manner, and consistent with payment card security requirements such as the PCI DSS.

Similarly, there are detailed and specific rules that apply to both pre-authorisations and to recurring payments. These include ensuring at the outset clear customer agreement to, and understanding of, the possible future payment transactions these may permit, including the amount and frequency of payments and ongoing information and receipt requirements.

Transport operators, and their payment service providers, will need to work through their specific models and processes for taking payment in some detail in order to ensure these are compliant, and practical, for the particular transport, passenger and ticketing scenario.

It is, however, clear that in order to encourage greater uptake of public transport and reduce individual journeys, in turn reducing carbon and other harmful emissions, a seamless and barrier-free payment system is key. The easier it is for customers to pay for travel the more people in urban areas are likely to use it. The more public transport systems that adopt such systems the greater the volume of people will make the modal shift to public transport. This will only have a positive impact on the environment. Payment systems will be a catalyst in making public transport systems part of the solution for achieving net zero targets, and more cities across the globe should be looking to adopt them.

Transport operators, and their payment service providers, will need to work through their specific models and processes for taking payment in some detail in order to ensure these are compliant, and practical, for the particular transport, passenger and ticketing scenario.

Notes

1 Department for Transport (DfT), "Decarbonising Transport: A Better, Greener Britain", 2021, https://assets.publishing.service.gov.uk/government/uploads/system/uploads/attachment_data/file/1009448/decarbonising-transport-a-better-greener-britain.pdf.
2 SI 2017 No 752.
3 Directive (EU) 2015/2366 of the European Parliament and of the Council of 25 November 2015 on payment services in the internal market, amending Directives 2002/65/EC, 2009/110/EC and 2013/36/EU and Regulation (EU) No 1093/2010, and repealing Directive 2007/64/EC, https://eur-lex.europa.eu/legal-content/EN/TXT/?uri=CELEX:32015L2366.
4 Note that the PSRs are currently under review by the UK government as at the time of writing (following the publication of its Payment Services Regulations Review and Call for Evidence in January 2023), and the UK government is expected to make further announcements during the course of 2024 about its plans to replace the PSRs and EMRs as part of its Future Regulatory Framework Review, see www.fca.org.uk/publications/corporate-documents/future-regulatory-framework-review-reforms.
5 SI 2011 No 99.
6 SI 2015 No 2038.
7 Regulation (EU) No 260/2012 of the European Parliament and of the Council of 14 March 2012 establishing technical and business requirements for credit transfers and direct debits in euro and amending Regulation (EC) No 924/2009, https://eur-lex.europa.eu/legal-content/EN/TXT/?uri=CELEX:32012R0260.
8 Regulation (EU) 2019/518 of the European Parliament and of the Council of 19 March 2019 amending Regulation (EC) No 924/2009 as regards certain charges on cross-border payments in the Union and currency conversion charges, https://eur-lex.europa.eu/legal-content/EN/TXT/?uri=CELEX:32019R0518.
9 Regulation (EU) 2015/751 of the European Parliament and of the Council of 29 April 2015 on interchange fees for card-based payment transactions, https://eur-lex.europa.eu/legal-content/EN/TXT/?uri=CELEX:32015R0751.
10 Money Laundering, Terrorist Financing and Transfer of Funds (Information on the Payer) Regulations 2017 (SI 2017 No 692).
11 Regulation (EU) 2015/847 of the European Parliament and of the Council of 20 May 2015 on information accompanying transfers of funds and repealing Regulation (EC) No 1781/2006, https://eur-lex.europa.eu/legal-content/EN/TXT/?uri=CELEX:32015R0847.
12 Regulation (EU) 2016/679 of the European Parliament and of the Council of 27 April 2016 on the

protection of natural persons with regard to the processing of personal data and on the free movement of such data, and repealing Directive 95/46/EC (General Data Protection Regulation), https://eur-lex.europa.eu/legal-content/EN/TXT/?uri=CELEX:32016R0679.
13 Payment Card Industry Security Standards Council, "Payment Card Industry Data Security Standard (PCI DSS)", Version 3.2.1 (2018), www.pcisecuritystandards.org/document_library?document=pci_dss.
14 UK Finance, "Contactless Transit EMV Framework", December 2017, www.ukfinance.org.uk/system/files/UK-Finance-Contactless-Transit-EMV-Framework.pdf.
15 See, eg, regulation 67 of the Payment Services Regulations 2017.

V. Connected autonomous vehicles: the future of mobility and their role in achieving net zero

Charles Christie
Nathalie Moreno
William Smith
Addleshaw Goddard

1. Introduction

The automotive industry is undergoing a revolutionary transformation, propelled by advancements in technology and the pursuit of safer, more efficient transportation. At the forefront of this transformation are connected autonomous vehicles (CAVs), which combine the power of connectivity, artificial intelligence and automation to redefine the driving experience.

In this chapter, we will look at the potential of CAVs, the existing legislative landscape and the work needed to be done to allow the widespread introduction of CAVs on public highways.

2. Understanding connected autonomous vehicles

CAVs are vehicles equipped with advanced technologies that enable them to operate without human intervention, using a combination of sensors, cameras, radar systems and sophisticated algorithms in combination, to enable a CAV to understand its immediate surrounding environment sufficiently such that it can determine the calculated risks and make appropriate 'decisions' accordingly.

CAVs communicate with their surroundings, including other vehicles, infrastructure, and even pedestrians, through wireless connectivity. The Occupational Road Safety Association reports that 94% of road traffic incidents are attributable to human error. A significant 42% of the 118,404 UK road traffic incidents analysed by British police in 2011 were caused by a driver failing to look properly. A further 21% were caused by a driver failing to judge the other vehicle's speed and path.[1] It is widely understood that the introduction of CAVs would remove this element of human error from the driving activity in favour of a form of artificial intelligence which would determine calculated actions based on the surrounding environment and known variables such as weather. In theory this will be a significant step towards enhancing safety on the roads.

3. Self-driving and levels of automation

The level of automation of a CAV can differ greatly, and some vehicles will be advertised as having autonomous vehicle capabilities without really being capable of driving without a human. Indeed, in response to investigations by the US National Highway Traffic Safety Administration and the Securities Exchange Commission in 2022 a class action was brought by drivers against Tesla for overstating the company's 'Autopilot' technology. This was followed by a claim by Tesla shareholders in February 2023 when the Tesla share price fell 5.7% on 16 February 2023 following the recall of Tesla vehicles instigated by the US National Highway Traffic Safety Administration.

To provide a clear framework for categorising the various levels of automation in vehicles, The Society of Automotive Engineers established the classification system that we've adapted in Table 1.

4. Benefits of connected autonomous vehicles

CAVs offer an array of capabilities that can revolutionise the way we travel:

- *Enhanced safety:* CAVs leverage advanced sensor systems and artificial intelligence algorithms to continuously monitor their surroundings, detecting potential risks and reacting faster than human drivers. They can mitigate accidents caused by human errors, such as distracted driving or fatigue.
- *Improved efficiency:* By leveraging real-time data and communication with other vehicles and infrastructure, CAVs optimise traffic flow, reducing congestion and improving fuel efficiency. They can also choose the most efficient routes based on traffic conditions and environmental factors.
- *Intelligent navigation:* Connected features allow CAVs to access up-to-date mapping and traffic information, enabling them to make informed decisions about the best routes and avoid road closures or traffic jams. This results in faster and smoother journeys.
- *Seamless connectivity:* CAVs enable passengers to stay

Table 1: Levels of automation in vehicles

Level 0	No automation	At this level, the vehicle is entirely controlled by a human driver, with no automated assistance or features.
Level 1	Driver assistance	Level 1 introduces basic automation features, such as cruise control or lane-keeping assistance, which can assist the driver but still require their continuous attention and control.
Level 2	Partial automation	Vehicles at this level offer more advanced driver-assistance systems, capable of simultaneously controlling steering, acceleration and braking under certain conditions. However, the driver is still responsible for monitoring the driving environment.
Level 3	Conditional automation	Level 3 vehicles can take full control of the driving task under specific conditions and environments, allowing the driver to disengage from actively monitoring the vehicle. However, the driver must be ready to resume control when prompted by the vehicle.
Level 4	High automation	At this level, the vehicle can perform all driving functions under predetermined conditions and environments without requiring any human intervention. However, a human driver can still take control if needed.
Level 5	Full automation	Level 5 represents the pinnacle of automation, where vehicles are fully capable of operating independently without any human interaction, regardless of the environment or driving conditions.

Source: Table created by authors based on The Society of Automotive Engineers classification system.[2]

connected to the digital world while on the move. With integrated infotainment systems, passengers can access entertainment, productivity tools and stay connected to their devices, enhancing the overall travel experience. This connectivity even extends to the ability for vehicle users to make payments (whether for parking, road tolls or even cinema and theatre tickets) electronically via the vehicle – much like contactless payments on mobile phone devices today.

- *Eco-friendly transportation:* The advanced algorithms and connectivity in CAVs enable efficient energy management. They can optimise speed, acceleration and braking, reducing fuel consumption and emissions, thereby contributing to a greener future.

5. Connected autonomous vehicles and net zero

Specifically, the adoption of CAVs can play a significant role in supporting the push for net zero mobility. Ways in which CAVs can contribute to achieving a transport system with minimal or no greenhouse gas (GHG) emissions include:

- *Electrification:* CAVs are often designed with electric or hybrid powertrains, reducing or eliminating reliance on fossil fuels. Electric vehicles (EVs) produce zero tailpipe emissions and, when coupled with renewable energy sources (for use in both the manufacturing process and the powering of the CAV), they offer a cleaner and greener alternative to traditional internal combustion engine (ICE) vehicles. CAVs can accelerate the transition to electric mobility by driving demand for EVs and supporting the expansion of charging infrastructure.
- *Efficiency and traffic optimisation:* CAVs can optimise traffic flow and reduce congestion through advanced communication and coordination between vehicles. By leveraging real-time data, CAVs can choose the most efficient routes, adjust speeds to minimise stop-and-go traffic and optimise energy consumption. This leads to reduced fuel consumption and emissions, making transportation more environmentally friendly.
- *Eco-driving and energy management:* CAVs can employ advanced algorithms and predictive analytics to optimise energy management. By analysing factors such as traffic conditions, road topography and weather patterns, CAVs can optimise acceleration, deceleration and cruising speeds to maximise energy efficiency. This eco-driving approach helps minimise energy waste and reduce emissions.
- *Modal shift and shared mobility:* CAVs can facilitate a shift from individual car ownership to shared mobility models. By providing convenient, on-demand transportation, CAVs can encourage people to use shared services like ride-hailing and carpooling. Shared mobility reduces the overall number of vehicles on the road, leading to lower emissions and overall improved resource utilisation.
- *Intelligent infrastructure integration:* CAVs can interact with smart infrastructure to enhance efficiency and sustainability. For instance, they can communicate with traffic signal systems to optimise signal timings, reducing idle times and congestion. CAVs can also utilise infrastructure-integrated charging stations,

CAVs can encourage people to use shared services like ride-hailing and carpooling. Shared mobility reduces the overall number of vehicles on the road, leading to lower emissions and overall improved resource utilisation.

allowing for more efficient charging and grid integration, further promoting renewable energy adoption.

- *Integration with multi-modal transport:* CAVs can seamlessly integrate with other modes of transportation, such as public transit and cycling infrastructure. By providing last-mile connectivity and improving accessibility to public transportation, CAVs can encourage more people to use sustainable modes of travel, reducing the reliance on private cars and lowering emissions.
- *Data-driven planning and policymaking:* CAVs generate vast amounts of data related to traffic patterns, vehicle usage and energy consumption. This data can inform urban planning, infrastructure development and transportation policies. By leveraging this data, cities and policymakers can make informed decisions to optimise transportation systems, promote sustainable practices and create policies that align with net zero mobility objectives.

The adoption of CAVs has the potential to contribute significantly to the transition towards net zero mobility. The collective benefits outlined above contribute to reducing emissions and building a more sustainable and environmentally friendly transportation system.

6. Legal imperative and the current regulatory landscape

There is no legal imperative to introduce CAVs onto public highways, but the benefit of doing so (outlined in sections 4 and 5 above) is compelling. Many countries around the globe (from the UK to the UAE) have been piloting CAV technologies. Turning first to the UK, the government has been actively working to establish a legal framework to support the introduction of CAVs and pave the way for their safe and widespread deployment. To facilitate the development and deployment of CAVs, several key legislative initiatives have been put in place. The primary components of the current legal framework supporting CAVs in the UK include:

- *Automated Vehicles Act 2024:* This new piece of legislation was passed by parliament in May 2024 with the purpose of implementing the key recommendations for a regulatory framework for CAVs from the joint report from Law Commission of England and Wales and the Scottish Law Commission. This is discussed in detail below.
- *Automated and Electric Vehicles Act 2018:* This legislation focuses on facilitating the use of CAVs on UK roads. It establishes a framework for insurance coverage by ensuring that both the CAV's owner and the CAV's insurer are liable for accidents caused by the CAV's automated driving functions. It also empowers the government to set minimum cybersecurity standards for CAVs to ensure their safety and resilience against potential cyber threats.
- *Code of Practice for automated vehicle trialling:* The UK government published a Code of Practice for those involved in testing CAVs on public roads. The code provides guidelines and safety standards for CAV testing, ensuring that testing is conducted in a controlled manner that minimises risks to public safety. It encourages collaboration between CAV developers, local authorities and other stakeholders to ensure proper evaluation and validation of CAV technologies.
- *Future of Mobility: Urban Strategy:* The UK government's Future of Mobility: Urban Strategy, (published by the Department for Transport (DfT) in March 2019)[3] outlines its vision for transforming urban mobility, including the deployment of CAVs. The strategy emphasises the importance of developing an enabling regulatory framework that promotes innovation, ensures safety and addresses the impact of CAVs on cities and transportation systems.
- *Centre for Connected and Autonomous Vehicles (CCAV):* Established as long ago as 2015, the CCAV is a joint initiative of the DfT and what was the Department for Business, Energy and Industrial Strategy (now the Department for Energy Security and Net Zero and the Department for Science, Innovation and

Technology). The CCAV plays a crucial role in supporting the development and deployment of CAVs in the UK – working closely with industry, academia and local authorities to foster innovation, to provide funding support for CAV-related projects and engaging in policy development.

The UK government continues to work closely with industry stakeholders, experts and the public to address emerging challenges, refine regulations and ensure the safe integration of CAVs into the transportation ecosystem.

An example of UK government's engagement with industry stakeholders – and testament to the continuing evolution of the UK's legal framework for CAVs – is the call for evidence in relation to the safe use of Automated Lane Keeping System (ALKS)[4] which was conducted by the DfT and CCAV in 2020. The purpose was to gather feedback and insights on the regulatory framework for the use of ALKS on British roads.

ALKS is a specific type of advanced driver assistance system that can take control of the vehicle's steering to keep it within its lane at speeds up to 60km/h (37mph) on highways or dual carriageways. The United Nations Economic Commission for Europe (of which the UK is a member) approved the technical requirements for ALKS in June 2020.

The UK government continues to work closely with industry stakeholders, experts and the public to address emerging challenges, refine regulations and ensure the safe integration of CAVs into the transportation ecosystem.

The call for evidence aimed to gather public and industry opinions on proposed amendments to the existing regulatory framework to enable the safe use of ALKS. The key areas covered in the call for evidence included the following:

- *The definition of ALKS:* The call for evidence sought feedback on the proposed definition of ALKS, its capabilities and its limitations. This was essential to establish a clear understanding of the system and ensure consistent implementation across manufacturers and vehicle models.
- *Approval process and safety requirements:* The call for evidence explored the appropriate approval process and safety requirements for ALKS. This included considerations such as type approval, technical specifications and safety performance standards to ensure that ALKS-equipped vehicles meet the required safety levels.
- *Monitoring and compliance:* The call for evidence sought input on the monitoring and compliance mechanisms for ALKS. This involved questions regarding the need for data recording and logging, remote monitoring and ensuring that the system functions as intended throughout its lifecycle.
- *Driver responsibilities and handover times:* The call for evidence addressed the roles and responsibilities of drivers while using ALKS. It included questions on driver attentiveness, appropriate handover times between the system and the driver, and whether the driver should maintain a legal responsibility for the vehicle's actions.
- *Public information and user guidance:* The call for evidence explored the provision of accurate and clear information to the public regarding the capabilities and limitations of ALKS. It sought feedback on the best approaches to educate drivers and users about the safe use of the technology.

The call for evidence process allowed stakeholders, including manufacturers, road safety organisations, consumer groups and the general public, to provide their views, concerns and recommendations on these key aspects. The DfT aimed to use the feedback received to shape the regulatory framework for ALKS and ensure the safe and efficient integration of this technology into the UK's road network.

In June 2020, the United Nations Economic Committee introduced regulation around the use of ALKS which took effect in 2020. In 2022 after further consultation the UK introduced new rules on the safe use of automated vehicles in the UK, which resulted in updates to the Highway Code.[5]

Clear guidelines and regulations for data collection, sharing and usage are required to build trust and confidence in the global CAV ecosystem.

It is worth noting that the implementation of the regulatory changes and the deployment of ALKS on UK roads are ongoing processes, and further updates and developments may occur in the future as the technology evolves and safety requirements are refined.

7. How do we get there?

While there are some nascent regulations starting to form the path for the widespread introduction of CAVs as described above, to enable the full adoption of CAVs, several key actions and considerations need to be addressed:

- *Regulatory framework (including data governance and security):* The UK needs to establish a comprehensive regulatory framework that addresses the specific requirements clear and challenges posed by CAVs. This includes defining the legal responsibilities of manufacturers, operators and vehicle users, as well as ensuring safety standards, cybersecurity measures and data protection protocols. Such a regulatory framework must include robust data governance and security measures as these are essential to protect the privacy of individuals, ensure data integrity and prevent unauthorised access to CAV-related information. Clear guidelines and regulations for data collection, sharing and usage are required to build trust and confidence in the global CAV ecosystem. We look at developments in the legal framework in various jurisdictions in more detail below.

- *Infrastructure readiness:* The nature of enabling infrastructure required for the roll-out of CAVs very much depends on the nature of the CAV. It may be helpful for an increased number of charging stations to be deployed for electric CAVs. Air-based vehicles, however, will also require appropriate launch and landing infrastructure. Similarly, implementing intelligent transportation systems (ITS) infrastructure (consisting of fibreoptic communications systems and 5G WiFi coverage) for robust connectivity and data exchange capabilities between vehicles and infrastructure could well enhance the capabilities and ultimately the safety of CAVs. Many of the CAVs in trials or operation around the world, though, are working on the infrastructure already in place – so it is possible for this technology to operate with the infrastructure systems we have in place today. For example, Cruise has been granted a licence by the Dubai Roads and Transport Authority to run a robotaxi trial in Dubai, UAE.[6]
- *Testing, validation and setting the standards:* Continued testing and validation of CAVs are crucial to ensure their safety, reliability and compliance with regulatory standards.

Collaborating with industry leaders, academia and international organisations can help align regulations, standards and best practices, ensuring interoperability and facilitating the global adoption of CAV technologies.

Collaborating with industry leaders, academia and international organisations can help align regulations, standards and best practices, ensuring interoperability and facilitating the global adoption of CAV technologies. Industry needs to be part of the development of testing, validation and safety standards. Being a 'first-mover' nation will more likely result in other countries adopting these standards as the international benchmark. The likes of vehicle testing agency, HoribaMIRA in the UK, are actively developing models and standards for testing CAV technologies. Many of these technologies can be tested and verified in a virtual environment – reducing (if not removing) the need for testing on the track or public roads. This, in turn, means CAV capabilities can be brought to market quicker than traditional automotive testing, and intrinsically reduces the development and testing costs of autonomous technologies which would otherwise be a prohibitive barrier to entry. Such testing facilities and methodologies need to be supported by governments in order to allow the industry to develop its solutions.

- *Skill development and workforce transition:* Much like the transition from internal combustion engine to electric vehicles, the introduction of CAVs (which will most likely be powered by electricity or alternative sustainable fuels) requires a skilled workforce capable of designing, developing, maintaining and operating these advanced vehicles. Governments – in conjunction with industry – will need to invest in training programmes, education initiatives and research and development activities to nurture talent and prepare the workforce for the emerging CAV industry.
- *Public acceptance and trust:* Building public acceptance and trust in CAVs is essential. Engaging in public outreach campaigns, education programmes and initiatives to address concerns related to safety, data privacy and job displacement will be key for any government looking to introduce CAVs as part of the transport system. The safety benefits are compelling when looking at the statistics discussed earlier in this chapter, but public concerns over the perceived risks associated with data security may be harder to alleviate.
- *Policy and Incentives:* Introducing policies and incentives to promote the adoption of CAVs could be a useful tool for governments to encourage uptake of CAV usage. This includes measures such as tax incentives for electric and autonomous vehicles, grants for research and development and supportive policies that encourage CAV deployment (eg, allowing CAVs in certain lanes or designated areas). Such policies would need to be fully thought through, as unlike regular EVs where a grant to discount the purchase price of a new EV would encourage

potential purchasers to make the jump, the early use cases for CAVs are likely to be ride shares – where vehicle ownership is not actually the focus.

By addressing these areas, countries can create an environment that fosters the safe and efficient adoption of CAVs, leading to improved road safety, enhanced mobility, reduced congestion and a more sustainable transportation system.

8. The direction of travel across the globe

8.1 United Kingdom

The Law Commission of England and Wales and the Scottish Law Commission jointly issued a consultation in 2020 to gather the views on implementing a regulatory framework for CAVs, which included proposals around standards and liability, as well as the governance of personal data.[7] In May 2024, parliament passed the Automated Vehicles Act 2024 putting these recommendations in place and empowering the secretary of state to develop and impose requirements that implement the regulations. The key areas are described below:

(a) Registration and approval process

The vehicle manufacturer, or the technology company putting forward a vehicle for authorisation as an autonomous vehicle, will be the authorised self-driving entity (ASDE) and will be responsible for ensuring CAVs are always compliant with British traffic laws, respond to regulatory action and organise a recall should issues arise. The ASDE must demonstrate it was closely involved in assessing the safety of the CAV and be of good repute, suitable financial standing and capable of competently discharging any authorisation requirements imposed on it.

A CAV will need to obtain type approval either from the existing United Nations Economic Commission for Europe or from the new UK-specific approval scheme operated by the Vehicle Certification Agency. In each case, the vehicle type must achieve the new GB Whole Vehicle Approval (replacing the EU Whole Vehicle Approval).

Having gained type-approval, a CAV will need to be authorised to drive itself (and doesn't simply have driver assistance) to distinguish between CAVs and regular vehicles for legal purposes. This process includes:

- a safety case (a nominated person within the ASDE would be responsible for this and face criminal sanctions if they failed to exercise due diligence to ensure that the information submitted was correct and complete);

- an equality impact assessment (demonstrating that the technology has been adequately tested taking into account the needs of vehicle users and others on the road to ensure that no one is treated unequally on the basis of protected characteristics); and
- explaining how data will be recorded, stored, accessed and protected.

The secretary of state will be obliged to keep a public register of all automated vehicle authorisations granted, and to establish proportionate monitoring of the performance of authorised CAVs.

(b) On the road

There will be an 'in-use safety' regulator (possibly the existing Driver and Vehicle Standards Agency) to ensure the continuing safety and legal compliance of CAVs while in use. It will have powers to impose regulatory sanctions. The regulator will be empowered to collect safety data and compare this against the safety standard set by UK government.

While 'users-in-charge' (the human in the driving seat while a self-driving feature is engaged) of a CAV are able to engage in other activities when the CAV is driving, they will:

There will be an 'in-use safety' regulator (possibly the existing Driver and Vehicle Standards Agency) to ensure the continuing safety and legal compliance of CAVs while in use. It will have powers to impose regulatory sanctions. The regulator will be empowered to collect safety data and compare this against the safety standard set by UK government.

- only be able to use a screen for non-driving activities if it cuts out at the start of a 'transition demand' (a request from the vehicle to hand control of the vehicle back to the user-in-charge); and
- not be allowed to sleep in the CAV while it is self-driving.

The police will continue to levy traffic infractions (such as speeding tickets) against the registered owner of a vehicle. Such an owner would need to inform the police if the vehicle was in autonomous mode at the time of the infraction (presumably with evidence of the same). Once established that this was the case, the in-use regulator would investigate and resolve the issue.

A specialist independent investigator should be established to investigate road collisions involving CAVs. It makes sense that this would be the same Road Collision Investigation Branch proposed to be formed by the RAC, as many collisions will include non-autonomous vehicles.

No additional mandatory training will be imposed on drivers/users-in-charge for using a CAV on the assumption that these will be intuitive. A user-in-charge must, however, be fit and qualified to drive, meaning they must have a valid driving licence and must not be under the influence of alcohol or illegal substances. It would become a criminal offence to be in charge of a CAV while unfit or unqualified as it is for a conventional vehicle.

(c) Liability of user-in-charge

While a CAV is in autonomous or self-driving mode, the user-in-charge will be immune from liability for traffic law infractions.

Once there has been a completed handover of control from the CAV back to the user-in-charge, the user-in-charge would become a driver of the CAV and the existing road rules and laws would apply as for conventional vehicles. The exception to this will be for infractions occurring immediately after a handover of control, where the CAV caused the infraction, and a competent and careful driver could not have avoided it.

Failing to respond to a transition demand/notification of handing over control by the CAV will be an offence, and the driver's immunity from responsibility for the CAV shall cease from the point where control is handed back. Failing to respond to such an instruction may result in the CAV coming to a stop in the road which would cause a hazard to other road-users. This would be a criminal offence akin to 'driving without due care and attention'.

The Automated Vehicles Act 2024 envisages that further clarifications will need to be made to existing traffic laws to account for the development of CAV technology and the concept of a user-in-charge.

(d) Driverless CAVS

For operations of a CAV where no user-in-charge (NUIC) is present in the CAV, a remote operator (NUIC operator) should have oversight of the CAV's activities. The NUIC operator must respond to alerts from the CAV if it encounters a problem it cannot resolve, breaks down or is involved in a collision.

The Automated Vehicles Act 2024 grants the secretary of state to introduce licence requirements for a NUIC operator. A NUIC operator must be licenced by a regulating body (possibly the Vehicle Certification Agency) having demonstrated it is of good repute, has appropriate financial standing, conducts its operations within Great Britain and is professionally competent to run the service. The application process includes:

- submitting a safety case; and
- explaining how it will maintain connectivity, train and supervise staff, avoid staff becoming bored and inattentive from simply viewing the autonomous activities of the CAV.

It is likely that the ASDE and the NUIC operator will be the same entity.

(e) Liability of ASDE and NUIC

The CAV liability regime for ASDEs and NUICs is based on the 'duty of candour'. It is a criminal offence for the ASDE or NUIC operator to: (i) fail to provide information to the regulator; or (ii) provide information to the regulator that is false or misleading, in each case where that information is relevant to the evaluation of the safety of the CAV. The only defence would be demonstrating it took reasonable precautions and exercised all due diligence to prevent the wrongdoing.

Those who play a significant role in:

- the making of decisions about how the ASDE or NUIC operator is managed or organised; or
- the management of the safety assurance process,

will have the potential for criminal liability if an offence took place with their 'consent or connivance', that is, turning a blind-eye to the wrongdoing.

The nominated person signing the safety case submitted as part of the registration process must demonstrate they have taken active steps to ensure that the information submitted to the regulator is correct and complete. The only defence for such nominated person is to establish that on the balance of possibilities they took reasonable precautions and exercised all due diligence to prevent the wrongdoing.

A three-part test is proposed where a senior manager or corporation has committed an offence. That offence will be aggravated where the misrepresentation or non-disclosure:

- related to an increased risk of a type of adverse incident;
- an adverse incident of that type occurred; and
- the adverse incident caused a death or serious injury.

The Automated Vehicles Act 2024 also empowers the secretary of state to impose civil sanctions on each of the ASDE and NUIC Operator where a traffic infraction occurred while the CAV was in its control. Such action may include financial penalties being levied or requiring that certain actions are taken.

(f) Uninsured CAVs

The Law Commission recommended that the protections provided by the Motor Insurer's Bureau as insurer of last resort to victims of uninsured vehicles should be extended to uninsured CAVs.

The Automated Vehicles Act 2024 also empowers the secretary of state to impose civil sanctions on each of the ASDE and NUIC Operator where a traffic infraction occurred while the CAV was in its control. Such action may include financial penalties being levied or requiring that certain actions are taken.

(g) Application of legacy European Union data legislation and guidance in the UK

EDPB 2021 Guidelines on connected vehicles: On 9 March 2021, the European Data Protection Board (EDPB) published its Guidelines on processing personal data in the context of CAVs (Guidelines 1/2020)[8] (Guidelines). These Guidelines aim to provide some much-needed guidance and clarity surround the processing of personal data in CAVs in the wake of the ITS Directive.[9] It is primarily aimed at car manufacturers and providers of services in the connected vehicles ecosystem.

The Guidelines specifically cover personal data:

- processed inside the vehicle;
- exchanged between the vehicle and personal devices (ie, the user's smartphone); or
- collected locally in the vehicle and exported to external entitles (ie, vehicle manufacturers and insurance companies).

(h) Application of existing data protection laws on CAVs

UK data protection issues: Much of the data generated by CAVs is likely to identify individual users and will be considered to be their 'personal data' unless anonymised. This means that it falls within scope of the GDPR (as enacted into UK law) (UK GDPR).[10] The UK GDPR applies to UK organisations and non-UK organisations targeting the UK market that are data 'controllers' and requires them (amongst other things) to:

- ensure they have a lawful basis to process personal data (eg, consent, contract necessity or legitimate interest);
- provide necessary privacy information to the affected individuals or 'data subjects';
- only process personal data for specified limited purposes;
- minimise personal data to what is necessary (and design processes to minimise the use of personal data by default);
- ensure personal data is accurate and kept up to date;
- only store personal data for a reasonable period;
- keep personal data secure; and
- enable data subjects to exercise their rights in relation to their personal data.

Controllers are those persons or organisations which control and determine the means and purposes of collecting and using personal data. Limited obligations also apply to 'processors' such as service providers who may process personal data on their behalf.

Personal data likely to be processed by CAVs includes data directly identifying individuals, such as complete driver profiles, as well as indirectly identifiable data like journey details and location data, vehicle usage data (eg, driving habits or mileage), or vehicle technical data (eg, part wear and tear information), which can be linked to individuals when cross-referenced with the vehicle identification number. Personal data processed by CAVs may also include metadata like vehicle maintenance status. In the event of an incident, CAVs may also collect data related specifically to that incident, including timestamps and potentially video/audio.

The use of CAVs raises various data protection issues, due to the extensive volume of personal data generated and processed by these vehicles. There can also be potential challenges with determining who is responsible for the data. Manufacturers, insurers and car-sharing providers touching CAV data may all have obligations as controllers under the UK GDPR and must ensure they can comply.

This part of the chapter explores the main data protection concepts that are relevant in this context, including data ownership, privacy by design, data sharing, data minimisation, transparency, consumer choice and international data transfers. It also examines the expected 2025 response from the Information Commissioner's Office (ICO) pertaining to connected and automated mobility.

(i) Responsible parties

In a CAV context, there may be various parties with access to different sets of data, such as manufacturers, insurers and car-sharing providers, such as Uber or rental services such as Zipcar. This presents numerous legal complexities, including determining who defines the purposes and means of data processing and whether multiple entities may be acting jointly as 'joint controllers' or a party may be processing data on behalf of another as 'processor'.

Where multiple parties are involved, it will be necessary to establish who will be the interface with the data subjects and provide all the necessary privacy information. These relationships also need to be carefully documented with appropriate data protection provisions. As, for example, parties acting as joint controllers are required by Article 26 of the UK GDPR to have a transparent arrangement setting out their respective responsibilities for compliance with the UK GDPR. Article 28 of the GDPR also requires controllers to have a written contract with their processors with certain mandatory data protection terms which enable the controller to maintain oversight of the processor and ensure the secure processing of the data.

(j) Lawful basis

Connected vehicles are commonly defined as automobiles equipped with multiple electronic control units that are interconnected via an onboard network and communication features, enabling the sharing of information with devices both inside and outside the vehicle. Consequently, they fall under the category of terminal equipment as outlined in Article 1 of Directive 2008/63/EC, dated 20 June 2008.[11]

In addition to the UK GDPR, Directive 2002/58/EC, also known as the 'e-Privacy Directive'[12] establishes specific regulations to ensure the confidentiality of communications and safeguard the personal data of users in the electronic communications sector. It also safeguards the integrity of terminal equipment used by subscribers or users within the EU. This directive sets a specific standard for operators who intend to store or access information stored in a subscriber's or user's terminal equipment.

In light of the above, the EDPB determines that the legal basis for processing in CAVs is Article 5(3) of the e-Privacy Directive. This article mandates that controllers must obtain the consent of the user before processing their data, provided that: (i) the purpose of the processing is clearly and succinctly communicated to the concerned subscriber or user; and (ii) the user is given the option to object to such processing. It's important to note that this does not affect the possibility of technical storage or access, solely for the purpose of facilitating communication transmission or processing data in an

Connected vehicles are commonly defined as automobiles equipped with multiple electronic control units that are interconnected via an onboard network and communication features, enabling the sharing of information with devices both inside and outside the vehicle.

anonymous form. Under the EDPB Guidelines, it's widely accepted that consent prevails over legitimate interest processing as the main legal basis for the processing of vehicle data in the connected car ecosystem.

There are a number of issues with relying on consent as the lawful basis to process personal data in autonomous vehicles, one of those being processing personal data for a purpose other than for which the original consent had been given. This issue would become particularly prominent when disclosing personal data to insurance companies after an incident, or when offering driving behaviour-based insurance policies.

The EDPB advises that a way around this may be to aggregate the data shared with insurance companies and for manufacturers to not share the raw personal data. This could involve sharing numerical scores, that is, the force exerted on the brake pedal on a scale of 1–10 or the number of miles driven in any given month.

It's worth highlighting that, according to the EDPB, consent is the primary lawful basis for the storage or access to pre-existing information. Controllers can rely on other lawful bases, as stipulated in Article 6 of the UK GDPR, for subsequent and/or additional

While users generate extensive data through their interactions with the vehicle, manufacturers often collect and store this data and may seek to further commercialise that data.

processing operations. For instance, in the case of usage-based insurance, like 'pay-as-you-drive', insurance companies can base their processing activities on Article 6(1)(b) of the UK GDPR, provided they can establish both a valid contract with the data subject and the necessity of processing for the performance of that specific contract with the data subject.

(k) Data commercialisation

While users generate extensive data through their interactions with the vehicle, manufacturers often collect and store this data and may seek to further commercialise that data. Manufacturers would need to comply with their obligations to identify a lawful basis for their use of this data and to be transparent about all the use cases and provide all necessary privacy information. However, there are debates around the extent to which they can and should be allowed to do so at all, such as the Federation Internationale De L'Automobile's "My Car, My Data" campaign,[13] highlighting the need for drivers to have a choice regarding sharing their vehicle data.

It is not known to what extent these debates will lead to regulatory intervention in the UK, but it is clear that ownership and control of vehicle data is a crucial issue in the automotive industry and manufacturers and other service providers must be careful to ensure responsible, transparent and proportionate data use.

(l) Privacy by design

Privacy by design is a core principle requiring the incorporation of privacy considerations throughout the developmental lifecycle of CAVs. This means that manufacturers and service providers of autonomous vehicles must adopt a proactive stance on data protection when producing data processing technologies, ensuring that privacy features are integral to the technology's design and functionality – for example, by integrating robust security measures, anonymisation techniques, limiting data storage and building in user consent mechanisms from the outset.

A key feature of privacy by design would be to anonymise personal data at the point of collection, particularly when the data subject's identity is unnecessary for the intended purpose of data collection. The Centre for Data Ethics and Innovation's policy paper on responsible innovation in self-driving vehicles,[14] following consultations with manufacturers and technical experts, suggests that it should be feasible to anonymise all facial image data of other road users at the point of collection without adversely affecting the vehicle's function. In practice, implementing such features may prove challenging and require additional technical solutions, so this would need to be considered early in the development process.

(m) Data sharing between manufacturers and other parties

Where CAVs interact with various service providers and infrastructure, there is likely to be an element of data sharing. However, consumers may not fully appreciate the extent of the data collected about them, or understand what rights (if any) they have to selectively share or opt out of sharing their data.

An example of this could be location data; through this information third parties would be able to determine where a user works, where they live, where they shop, if they have any children, if they have any hobbies etc. All this information could be used to create personalised connections and target marketing messages at the user.

That said, any data sharing will need to be compliant with the UK GDPR, which includes: (i) identifying the lawful basis for the sharing and providing for opt-outs where required by law; (ii) informing the data subject of the data; and (iii) documenting the data sharing appropriately, with appropriate contractual terms and restrictions on the onward use and sharing of the information.

Another data sharing avenue to consider is data sharing with insurers, which is a particularly key issue as incident data will need to be shared with insurers to enable them to process claims under the Automated and Electric Vehicles Act 2018. However, there are data sharing initiatives with insurers that have been designed for other purposes, such as reducing the premium drivers pay on their insurance policy. Pay-as-you-drive is a type of usage-based insurance that tracks the driver's mileage and driving habits. Ultimately, safe driving will result in lower premiums. The EDPB has confirmed that the lawful basis for this type of data sharing would be consent, this would be differentiated into the e-Privacy Article 5(3) consent and Article 6 UK GDPR consent on the same basis that we have discussed above. The EDPB was also keen to clarify that this type of insurance should always be optional; the policy holder should always have a choice to sign up to a non-usage-based insurance policy.

The question remains as to what extent vehicle manufacturers should make connected car data available to third parties (eg, to enable other market participants to develop and offer comparable products and services). Under Regulation (EU) 2018/858,[15] manufacturers are obliged to do this to a certain extent in accordance with applicable data protection rules.

(n) Data minimisation

Another vital data protection principle that must be considered in this context is data minimisation. Data minimisation is a fundamental principle in CAVs. It involves limiting the collection and storage of

The question remains as to what extent vehicle manufacturers should make connected car data available to third parties (eg, to enable other market participants to develop and offer comparable products and services).

personal data to only what is necessary for the intended purpose. By doing so, the risk of data breaches and unauthorised access is reduced. This practice also ensures that individual privacy is protected, and data is used efficiently and responsibly.

Organisations involved in CAVs, such as vehicle manufacturers, equipment manufacturers and service providers, must carefully consider the categories of data they need from connected vehicles. They should only collect personal data that is relevant and necessary for the intended processing. For instance, sensitive data like location data, which can reveal a lot about individuals' habits, should only be collected if absolutely necessary.

When data needs to leave the vehicle, it is essential to consider anonymisation techniques. Anonymous information, which cannot be linked to an identified or identifiable person, is not subject to the UK GDPR. Anonymisation involves removing all identifiers from the data to the point that it cannot be retraced. Pseudonymisation, on the other hand, replaces directly identifying personal data with non-signifying pseudonyms. It is reversible and still considered as personal data under the UK GDPR. These techniques help reduce the risks associated with data processing.

CAV stakeholders should implement mechanisms that allow data subjects (ie, vehicle users) to have control over their data throughout the entire processing period. This includes tools for exercising rights such as access, rectification, erasure, restriction of processing, data portability and objection. Additionally, a profile management system within the vehicle can store user preferences and enable easy modifications to privacy settings. Vehicle users should have the ability to stop the collection of certain types of data, temporarily or permanently, unless specific legislation or critical vehicle functions dictate otherwise.

These practices are crucial in ensuring that data minimisation is upheld in the development and operation of autonomous vehicles, which often involve extensive data collection and processing.

(o) Transparency and the provision of a privacy notice

Under the UK GDPR, individuals have a fundamental right to be informed about the collection and use of their personal data. This information should be provided at the time when their personal data is collected. Moreover, data should not be processed in ways that data subjects would not reasonably expect. This is particularly crucial in the context of CAVs, where data subjects may include not only the vehicle owner but also other drivers, passengers and even pedestrians observed through the vehicle's sensor technology (eg, Tesla's external cameras capturing footage of the vehicle's surroundings when the

The unique challenges posed by CAVs require creative solutions to meet these privacy requirements effectively. CAVs often have limited physical interfaces, and this poses challenges in informing data subjects about the use of their personal data.

breaks are applied suddenly and interior cameras monitoring driver attentiveness).

This means that CAV users must have clear insight into the data collected and to understand their rights regarding the information they generate to make informed choices about their data. They must be fully informed about how their data is collected, processed and shared by both manufacturers and service providers. This extends to the algorithms used in CAVs and users should have clear insights into how decisions are made within the vehicle. To achieve this, a comprehensive privacy notice should be readily available and easily accessible to users. This notice should explain, in plain language, the data practices employed and provide users with the opportunity to make informed choices about their data.

The unique challenges posed by CAVs require creative solutions to meet these privacy requirements effectively. CAVs often have limited physical interfaces, and this poses challenges in informing data subjects about the use of their personal data. Unlike traditional products or services where privacy information can be displayed on websites or provided during purchase, CAVs may lack obvious ways to present privacy information. Manufacturers and service providers must find innovative ways to ensure that privacy information is effectively communicated to users and other relevant data subjects. The most likely solution will be using the vehicle human-machine interface console display at the beginning of each journey, or if the technology is available, on each passenger's personal mobile device on entering the vehicle before each journey.

(p) International data transfers

With CAVs operating across borders and vehicle manufacturers exporting into many global markets, international data transfers are inevitable. Under UK law, the current position surrounding international data transfers is that organisations must safeguard the transfers of personal data to countries without an adequacy decision (formal confirmation that such countries hold sufficiently developed protections for personal data) via the use of the International Data Transfer Agreement or UK Addendum (in conjunction with the EU Standard Contractual Clauses), if transfers are also likely to originate from the EU. There is also a requirement on the transferring party to undertake a transfer risk assessment, which assesses the laws of the recipient country and determines whether any of those laws cut across the rights of the data subjects whose personal data is being transferred.

Manufacturers and service providers must ensure that such data transfers comply with applicable data protection laws and standards.

As the realm of autonomous vehicles continues to evolve, addressing data protection implications remains a dynamic challenge. It necessitates cooperation between regulators, manufacturers, service providers and users to ensure that the potential of autonomous vehicles is realised responsibly while respecting individuals' privacy rights.

Implementing measures like standard contractual clauses or adhering to recognised privacy frameworks can help facilitate secure and compliant data transfers.

(q) Connected and Automated Mobility 2025 (ICO response)
The Information Commissioner's Office (ICO) response on connected and automated mobility, expected in 2025, will play a pivotal role in shaping data protection practices within the CAV industry. It is essential for manufacturers and service providers to be prepared to align their data practices with any regulatory guidelines or requirements put forth by the ICO to safeguard individuals' privacy rights effectively.

As the realm of autonomous vehicles continues to evolve, addressing data protection implications remains a dynamic challenge. It necessitates cooperation between regulators, manufacturers, service providers and users to ensure that the potential of autonomous vehicles is realised responsibly while respecting individuals' privacy rights. Through adherence to privacy by design principles, transparent data practices and user-centric frameworks, the future of CAVs can be a promising one, benefitting both the environment and the privacy of individuals.

8.2 European Union

(a) Liability

There is currently no EU-wide framework which solidifies rules on liability for damage caused by motor vehicles. Each member state currently regulates the liability of a driver (or user-in-charge in the case of a CAV). The January 2016 European Parliament Briefing on Automated Vehicles in the EU highlights that given that most EU legal regimes rely on causality to determine liability, vehicle automation presents new challenges as it can be difficult to establish causation and decide whether liability should be allocated to a defect with the vehicle itself (ie, product liability) or driver conduct.[16]

While the European Commission is working on numerous initiatives to harmonise EU-wide regulation of AV technical specifications, product safety, liability and insurance, there is no leading legislation in the EU which governs road traffic. Instead, this is dealt with at UN level by the 1968 Vienna Convention on Road Traffic which is ratified by all EU member states save for Spain. The Vienna Convention on Road Traffic was updated in July 2022 to apply also to CAVs.[17]

Where damage is caused by an incident while a CAV is in autonomous mode, existing regulation in the EU is likely to point to product liability laws (in particular the EU Product Liability Directive 85/374/EEC)[18] as the relevant legislation – however, this was not designed with autonomous vehicles in mind. The EU Product Liability Directive decrees that the producer of a product is liable for injuries caused by such defective product. A producer or manufacturer of a non-automated vehicle would not be liable for damage caused by such vehicle while it was under the control of a driver. However, where the activity of driving is no longer in the hands of a driver (or even the user-in-charge), then the manufacturer of the CAV will be liable for damage caused. They would then have to recover proportionately against their suppliers pursuant to the terms of any supply contracts in place. Given the complexities of the technology, it may be difficult for vehicle manufacturers to identify or prove that the part or system contributed by a supplier is at fault.

The EU Commission is proposing that CAVs are fitted with data recorders (akin to the 'black box' of an aircraft) to record and capture details around who was in control of the CAV at any given time – the user-in-charge or the CAV autonomous system. This would then be used to determine responsibility for damage caused by CAVs. In 2022, the EU Commission also introduced the proposal for an EU Artificial Intelligence Liability Directive[19] to harmonise the national rules on liability arising from damage caused by artificial intelligence across EU member states. If enacted, this directive would capture the use of CAV technology and simplify the process for bringing civil liability claims against AI developers and organisations utilising AI for any injuries or damage caused by AI products or services. The main purpose of this directive will be to place the providers of AI systems and products on equal footing in terms of product liability with those service and product providers within more tangible and traditional industries.

On a national level, many EU member states have started to develop their own independent legislation relating to liabilities surrounding CAVs. For example, Germany (home to many leading European vehicle manufacturers such as VW, Audi, BMW and Mercedes-Benz) has amended provisions of the German Road Traffic Act in 2017 to include new rules for CAV driving. The allocation of liability is relatively clear-cut in Germany where they operate a three-pillar model of potential responsible persons: (i) driver; (ii) owner; and (iii) manufacturer. Under German law, the driver/user-in-charge is seen as responsible for the act of driving and must monitor the CAV and intervene in the event of an emergency where there are semi-automated driving functions. If the driver fails to comply with their duties, thereby causing a road traffic incident, they are liable for resulting damage (alongside the owner of the CAV). The manufacturer may also be liable under product liability laws for damage caused by a defect in the CAV.

The insurance industry, however, takes a different view. According to insurers, the owner of the CAV (expected to be the insured party) would have to be liable even if they were not responsible for the driving activity – or indeed the action causing the damage. The insurance company would then pay for damages and potentially seek recourse from the manufacturer for failures to the driving system and controls if a product defect could be proven.

According to German law, for semi-autonomous vehicles (which include driver controls) the driver must be guilty of intent, negligence or any other misconduct for liability to be established for damage caused by an incident.

By contrast, Italy has a far less developed set of legislation relating to liabilities around CAVs. In 2018, Italy adopted the Smart Road Decree, which introduced rules for testing CAVs on public roads. It established an official authority, the Smart Road Observatory, to coordinate experiments, initiatives and research into CAVs. Until July 2022, Article 46 of the Italian Highway Code posed a huge obstacle to the deployment of CAVs as it defined vehicles as machines 'driven by a man' thereby dismissing the possibility of cars not being governed by humans. So, there is currently little coordination or consistency of regulation forming around CAVs – at least legislation is not developing at the same pace across the EU.

According to insurers, the owner of the CAV (expected to be the insured party) would have to be liable even if they were not responsible for the driving activity – or indeed the action causing the damage. The insurance company would then pay for damages and potentially seek recourse from the manufacturer for failures to the driving system and controls if a product defect could be proven.

(b) Data privacy

While the landscape in respect of data in the EU is very similar to that in the UK (largely due to the fact that the UK GDPR and EU GDPR mirror each other), there may be slight deviations in approach in each European country depending on how their data protection authority interprets the law.

That said, the European Commission is keen to facilitate the develop and roll out of CAVs across the EU and has supported their introduction and development on many different levels, including:

- policy initiatives;
- developing EU-wide standards;
- co-funding research and innovation projects; and
- developing EU legislation.

There have also been initiatives such as the 5G cross-border corridors, which allow vehicles to physically move across borders and where the cross-border road safety, data access, data quality and liability, connectivity and digital technologies can be tested and demonstrated.

8.3 China

China entered the autonomous vehicle arena in 2015, but comprehensive legislation for testing and deployment did not materialise until 2021 with the release of amendments to the Road Traffic Safety Law and the Regulations of Shenzhen Special Economic Zone on the Administration of Intelligent and Connected Vehicles. While these amendments provide a path for CAV integration, the regulatory landscape concerning liability remains vague.

(a) Liability

Shenzhen was the first region to introduce CAV-related legislation in the form of the Regulations of Shenzhen Special Economic Zone on the Administration of Intelligent and Connected Vehicles in June 2022. The Regulations set out responsibility in the event of an accident based on whether or not there is a driver/user-in-charge in the vehicle. If there is, then responsibility will sit with the driver/user-in-charge. If not, then the owner or manager of the vehicle will be liable for its actions.

If the damage and incident is caused by a defect in the CAV, then the manufacturer of the CAV will be held liable for such damage. In such cases, the driver, owner or manager of the CAV (as applicable) who

If the damage and incident is caused by a defect in the CAV, then the manufacturer of the CAV will be held liable for such damage. In such cases, the driver, owner or manager of the CAV (as applicable) who may have been initially found liable for the incident or infraction, would have to bring a claim against the manufacturer.

may have been initially found liable for the incident or infraction, would have to bring a claim against the manufacturer.

A slightly different approach has been developing in Shanghai, which in November 2022 introduced the Provisions of Shanghai Pudong New Area on Promoting Innovative Application of Driverless Intelligent Connected Vehicles. The laws are particularly vague. Rather than specifically outlining the categories of liability, the regulations state that traffic administrative department will determine liability in accordance with the laws, rules and regulations on road traffic safety. The starting point being that the owner of the CAV must first pay out damages and recover a contribution from any other responsible parties.

(b) Data privacy

In contrast, extensive regulations regarding data security are in place. Chinese privacy law defines 'personal data' broadly, encompassing details of passengers or drivers, location information, driving history, speed and more. Notably, all data, whether personal or categorised as 'important data', must be stored domestically, a unique requirement in China.

The stringent stance on data localisation raises challenges for data-dependent AVs, as it conflicts with the need for accurate digital maps, essential for autonomous navigation. China is actively developing additional regulations for cyber and data security in CAVs, including data security.

Additionally, draft rules in China require anonymisation or desensitisation of personal data in cases where obtaining consent is difficult. Drivers will likely have options to delete data collected within the vehicle. The process of taking Chinese data overseas, if necessary, will undergo rigorous security assessments.

8.4 United States

The United States has done very little at the federal level to introduce laws relating to autonomous vehicles. Although existing federal motor vehicle standards (eg, US Code Title 49, Subtitle VI, and Code of Federal Regulations Title 49, Subtitle B, Chapter V[20]) are applicable to all vehicles on the road, they were not formulated with CAVs in contemplation. The federal government, through agencies such as the National Highway Traffic Safety Administration, provides guidelines and safety standards for CAVs. While these guidelines aim to establish a baseline for safety and performance, they also influence how liability is assessed, particularly in terms of whether a CAV was compliant with federal standards at the time of an accident. In March 2023, the Autonomous Vehicle Industry Association released a set of federal policy recommendations to Congress and the US Department of Transportation regarding the safe deployment and commercial use of CAVs across the US,[21] but at the time of writing this is yet to be enacted into law. Much like the EU however, developments are being made on a state-by-state basis. As of May 2021, 38 US states had enacted legislation relating to CAVs. At the time of writing this Special Report, 20 of these states have established the requirements for CAV operators.[22]

(a) Liability

Traditionally, vehicle accidents have been governed by principles of negligence. However, with CAVs, determining liability can become more complicated. In cases where a CAV is involved in an accident, liability may shift from the driver to the manufacturer or other entities involved in the CAV's operation, under the principles of product liability. This is particularly relevant when a malfunction or flaw in the vehicle's autonomous systems is a contributing factor to the accident.

California – considered by many as the leading state for CAV development (and home to cities such as San Francisco which have been the home test beds for the likes of Cruise and robotaxi trials) – introduced a legal framework to govern the testing and deployment of CAVs. Article 3.7 and 3.8 of the California Vehicle Code gives the California Department of Motor Vehicles responsibility for registration and permitting of autonomous vehicles on California's roads.

In California as with many other US States, manufacturers of CAVs may be held liable under product liability law if it can be demonstrated that a defect in the vehicle's design, manufacturing process or software contributed to the accident. This includes scenarios where the autonomous driving system fails to perform as expected, leading to a collision. The challenge lies in proving that the defect was present and that it directly caused the damages or injuries incurred. In response to this position on liability, California requires the manufacturer to either maintain a US$5,000,000 insurance policy, bond or make cash deposit to the Department of Motor Vehicles as security for liabilities arising from testing the CAV on the road.

Liability may, however, also extend to software developers and third-party vendors who provide critical components or software for CAVs. If an accident is attributed to a software glitch or a failure in a component supplied by a third party, these entities could be held responsible for negligence or product liability.

States such as Florida[23] and Nevada[24] have introduced laws making it a defence for the manufacturer where: (i) the defect was caused by the original vehicle being converted by an unauthorised third party into a

CAV unless the defect causing injury was present in the vehicle as originally manufactured; or (ii) if equipment installed by the CAV technology manufacturer (as opposed to the vehicle OEM) was defective.

Arizona is another prominent state for CAV research and is home to Waymo and Cruise autonomous vehicles trials, yet the state has taken a different approach to CAV regulation than many others in the US. Arizona has far fewer regulations relating to CAVs and instead relies on general principles of negligence and product liability, as well as executive orders[25] prescribing certain actions. This includes mandating relevant authorities, for example, the Department of Transportation to take the necessary steps to support the testing and operation of fully autonomous vehicles on public roads. This light touch approach is understood to be intended to attract CAV manufacturers to establish manufacturing facilities in the state.

Without a national and organised approach to the development of the regulation, US states risk taking diverging approaches. For example, Florida and California have taken slightly different approaches in how they define the 'operator' of a CAV. In California, while it is acknowledged that a human may not need to be present in the vehicle,

Traditionally, vehicle accidents have been governed by principles of negligence. However, with CAVs, determining liability can become more complicated. In cases where a CAV is involved in an accident, liability may shift from the driver to the manufacturer or other entities involved in the CAV's operation, under the principles of product liability.

legislation focuses on the location of the human responsible for the operation of a CAV, defining 'operator' as "the person who is seated in the driver's seat, or, if there is no person in the driver's seat, causes the autonomous technology to engage".[26] By contrast, Florida takes a slightly more technology-centred approach, focusing on the capability of autonomous software systems rather than the role a human might play in their operation when it defines 'operator' as "any person who is in actual physical control of a motor vehicle upon the highway, or who is exercising control over or steering a vehicle being towed by a motor vehicle". Unsurprisingly, with no specific CAV regulation, Arizona doesn't even have a definition of 'operator'.

(b) Data privacy

In the United States, data privacy is governed by the Federal Trade Commission, alongside individual states that are crafting their own regulations, such as the California Consumer Privacy Act (CCPA), which includes some similar concepts and rights to UK GDPR, and serves as a benchmark for robust consumer protections concerning data ownership and privacy. Various states are enacting or considering privacy legislation, with Virginia and Colorado implementing new laws in 2023, and the California Privacy Rights Act which is also now in place.

Mobility companies in the US are tasked with making decisions about data privacy and security policies amid evolving federal and state regulations. Compliance with these regulations is essential for consumer protection while ensuring the commercial success of these organisations.

The CCPA sets stringent standards for consumer protection regarding data ownership and privacy, but as regulations continue to evolve in the US and globally, in-house counsel must stay vigilant and adapt policies to comply with new requirements.

8.5 UAE

The UAE is a federation of Emirates. Each of the seven member Emirates is permitted to maintain its own legislative body and judicial authority. There are specific matters which remain within the domain of the federal government (eg, foreign policy, defence etc), however, regulation of transport and technology can be conducted on an Emirate level. There is, therefore, potential for discrepancy in the development of laws.

(a) Liability

Dubai is the frontrunner within the UAE in terms of CAV regulation. Dubai's Roads and Transport Authority (RTA) has implemented the Dubai Autonomous Transportation Strategy which envisions that by

The law makes it illegal for an autonomous vehicle to operate on Dubai roads without being licenced to do so by the RTA and requires the CAV to be insured by an insurance company licensed to operate in Dubai.

2030, 25% of Dubai travel will be driverless.[27] Legislation was introduced for the first time in April 2023 in the form of Law No 9 of 2023 Regulating the Operation of Autonomous Vehicles in the Emirate of Dubai (which took effect in July 2023). This is also the first piece of legislation in the UAE to regulate the licensing, use and liability for CAVs. The law makes it illegal for an autonomous vehicle to operate on Dubai roads without being licenced to do so by the RTA and requires the CAV to be insured by an insurance company licensed to operate in Dubai.

There is much left to the discretion of the director general, but the Dubai law sets out various high-level obligations on an operator (the person authorised as such by the RTA). Such obligations include notifying the RTA of any accident the CAV is in and providing the RTA with any data it requests. The operator is liable for any damage to property or harm to individuals caused by the CAV in accordance with general civil liability laws in Dubai. The law refers defers to Federal Law No 21 of 1995 and Federal Law by Decree No 31 of 2021 in respect of criminal liabilities such that the operator of the CAV will be liable for acts committed by the CAV which constitute criminal acts, in the same way they would have been had they been driving a regular vehicle.

Unlike equivalent laws in other jurisdictions, the Dubai law does not make explicit provision for manufacturer liability. Instead, Article 12 includes obligations of an 'agent' (being a natural or legal person with whom rests the exclusive right to distribute CAVs under a commercial agency contract). The definition of an agent is likely to capture a distributor of CAVs within the UAE rather than the manufacturer (who typically has to partner with a local company in order to distribute vehicles in the Emirate), but this interpretation has not yet been tested in the courts.

An agent is obliged under the law to update and upgrade autonomous driving systems to cope with the updates made to the traffic and road systems and to ensure that the technical systems of CAVs are compatible with all technical systems of government entities concerned with roads and CAVs. Should damage caused by an incident be attributable to such agent failing to comply with its obligations then this would naturally give rise to it being liable for such damage.

It can, however, be difficult to determine who should be liable for damage caused by a CAV. This is further complicated in Dubai by Article 291 of the UAE Civil Transactions Law No 5 of 1985 which allows for liability to be apportioned between multiple persons where there are multiple contributors to the cause of damage.

(b) Data privacy

Regarding data protection in the UAE, the Federal Decree-Law No 45/2021, known as the Protection of Personal Data Law (PDPL), was issued in September 2021. It aims to regulate all data processing activities in the UAE, including some that occur beyond its borders. However, the implementation of PDPL awaits the issuance of its Executive Regulations, which will offer more detailed guidelines and obligations for data controllers. Until these regulations are released, the PDPL cannot be enforced. It is anticipated that organisations will have a grace period of six to 12 months following the publication of the Executive Regulations to ensure compliance with both PDPL 2021 and its accompanying requirements.

In addition to the PDPL, specific data protection laws apply within certain designated 'free zones' in the UAE. These zones are distinct economic areas that offer various benefits to businesses, including tax and customs advantages. Examples of such free zones include the Dubai International Finance Centre (DIFC), the Abu Dhabi Global Market and the Dubai Healthcare City. Within these zones, separate data protection regulations have been established, governing all businesses operating within their jurisdiction.

For instance, the DIFC operates under its own data protection law, known as DIFC Law No 5 of 2020 (DIFC DP Law), which has been effective since July 2020. This law applies to companies incorporated within the DIFC that handle personal data, whether within the zone or internationally. It may also extend to foreign entities processing personal data within the DIFC. The DIFC DP Law shares similarities with the GDPR but diverges in certain aspects, such as breach reporting requirements and the specific penalties that can be imposed. Oversight of compliance with the DIFC DP Law is managed by an independent regulator, the Office of the Commissioner of Data Protection.

9. Conclusion

As clean transportation advances to the use of autonomous vehicles, establishing a consistent international legal framework dealing with liability for damage caused by CAVs and addressing data protection challenges remains an essential piece of the jigsaw. Effective cooperation amongst regulators, manufacturers, service providers and users is crucial to harnessing the potential of autonomous vehicles responsibly while respecting individual privacy rights. By embracing principles of privacy by design, implementing transparent data practices and focusing on user-centric frameworks, the future of autonomous vehicles holds great promise for both environmental sustainability and the protection of individual privacy. The green credentials of CAVs and the potential they bring to taking people out of their own private vehicles (reducing the number of vehicles on the roads) means they could have a significant impact on global efforts to reach net zero by 2050.

Notes

1 ORSA, "Reducing Driver Error Accidents", www.orsa.org.uk/reducing-occupational-road-risk/reducing-driver-error-accidents. See also https://crashstats.nhtsa.dot.gov/Api/Public/ViewPublication/812115.
2 SAE International, "SAE J3016™ Levels of Driving Automation", www.sae.org/binaries/content/assets/cm/content/blog/sae-j3016-visual-chart_5.3.21.pdf.
3 Department of Transport (DfT), "Future of Mobility: Urban Strategy", March 2019, https://assets.publishing.service.gov.uk/media/5dcd8417ed915d071ca239e9/future-of-mobility-strategy.pdf.
4 GOV.UK, "Safe use of Automated Lane Keeping System on GB motorways: call for evidence", 18 August 2020, www.gov.uk/government/calls-for-evidence/safe-use-of-automated-lane-keeping-system-on-gb-motorways-call-for-evidence.
5 DfT, Consultation Outcome, "Rules on safe use of automated vehicles on GB roads", updated 25 April 2022, www.gov.uk/government/consultations/safe-use-rules-for-automated-vehicles-av/rules-on-safe-use-of-automated-vehicles-on-gb-roads.
6 Izzy Wood, "RTA and Cruise begin AV trial on Dubai roads", ADAS & Autonomous Vehicle International, 23 October 2023, www.autonomousvehicleinternational.com/news/robotaxis/rta-and-cruise-begin-av-trial-on-dubai-roads.html. See also www.rta.ae/links/sdt/en/index.html.
7 See https://lawcom.gov.uk/project/automated-vehicles/.
8 European Data Protection Board (EDPB), www.edpb.europa.eu/system/files/2021-03/edpb_guidelines_202001_connected_vehicles_v2.0_adopted_en.pdf.
9 Directive 2010/40/EU, https://eur-lex.europa.eu/legal-content/EN/TXT/?uri=CELEX%3A32023L2661.
10 See www.legislation.gov.uk/eur/2016/679/contents.
11 Directive 2008/63/EC, https://eur-lex.europa.eu/legal-content/EN/ALL/?uri=CELEX%3A32008L0063.
12 Directive 2002/58/EC, https://eur-lex.europa.eu/legal-content/EN/TXT/?uri=celex%3A32002L0058.

13 See https://mycarmydata.eu.
14 GOV.UK, "Responsible innovation in self-driving vehicles", 19 August 2022, www.gov.uk/government/publications/responsible-innovation-in-self-driving-vehicles.
15 Regulation (EU) 2018/858, https://eur-lex.europa.eu/legal-content/EN/TXT/?uri=celex%3A32018R0858#:~:text=Regulation%20(EU)%202018%2F858, No%20595%2F2009%20and%20repealing.
16 European Parliament, "Automated vehicles in the EU", January 2016, www.europarl.europa.eu/RegData/etudes/BRIE/2016/573902/EPRS_BRI(2016)573902_EN.pdf.
17 See https://treaties.un.org/doc/Publication/CN/2022/CN.26.2022-Eng.pdf.
18 See https://eur-lex.europa.eu/legal-content/EN/TXT/PDF/?uri=CELEX:31985L0374.
19 See www.europarl.europa.eu/RegData/etudes/BRIE/2023/739342/EPRS_BRI(2023)739342_EN.pdf.
20 See www.ecfr.gov/current/title-49/subtitle-B/chapter-V.
21 See https://theavindustry.org/policy#federal_policy.
22 Alabama, Arizona, Arkansas, California, Florida, Iowa, Kansas, Louisiana, Maine, Mississippi, Nevada, North Carolina, North Dakota, Oklahoma, Oregon, Tennessee, Texas, Utah, Vermont and West Virginia.
23 Chapter 316 of the 2015 Florida Statutes (Motor Vehicles).
24 Chapter 482A (Autonomous Vehicles) of the Nevada Revised Statutes.
25 Executive Order 2018-04 (Advancing Autonomous Vehicle Testing and Operating; Prioritizing Public Safety) https://azgovernor.gov/sites/default/files/related-docs/eo2018-04_1.pdf and www.azleg.gov/legtext/55leg/1R/summary/S.2813TAT.DOCX.htm#:~:text=Under%20the%20Executive%20Order%2C%20autonomous,safety%20laws%3B%20and%204)%20in.
26 California Code, Vehicle Code – VEH § 38750, https://codes.findlaw.com/ca/vehicle-code/veh-sect-38750/.
27 Dubai Roads and Transport Authority, "Dubai Self-Driving Transport Strategy & Roadmap", www.rta.ae/links/sdt/sdt-final.pdf.

VI. Green shipping

Ed Watt
Addleshaw Goddard

1. Introduction: the fuel choice dilemma

It is said that if the shipping industry were a nation state, it would be the eighth most polluting country in the world. In the United Kingdom, domestic shipping produces more greenhouse gases (GHG) than the emissions of the bus and rail modes together. The International Maritime Organization (IMO), the UN agency responsible for regulating shipping, recently set out plans for the shipping sector to reach net zero emissions by 2050.

With this blunt assessment, what is to be done? Zero emission fuels and vessels must move from demonstrator projects and prototypes to begin deployment at significant scale and number over the next decade to achieve full decarbonisation of the shipping sector by 2050. At present, no frontrunner for long duration deep sea transit has emerged. Which technologies will prevail? The critical green transition for the shipping industry faces unique challenges particularly around the issue of reliable bunkering (that is, refuelling) for the vessels of the chosen fuel type in the ports at both ends of the sea voyage. In addition, concerns about the continuing fuel-type suitability and the versatility of planned new vessels during their economic lifecycle over typically 25 years, continue to constrain investment decisions. Due to that long working life ahead, for maritime transport to reach net zero by the middle of this century, the newbuild fleet must be zero carbon by 2030.

For many ship owners and their financial backers, maintaining the maximum potential market for their vessels at the time of onwards sale in the secondary market is a key consideration as they place orders for newbuild tonnage today. This means there is a need for the vessels not just to be able to serve the ship owner's current routes, but to have ship technology that they know they can sell on – or with a proven capability for retrofitting of new technologies into an existing hull design – for alternative and wider medium- and long-term future use. As this takes place against a backdrop of rapid transformation of ports, fuel types and different new technologies, it can be difficult for ship owners and operators to make confident plans for the future. In many cases, vessel owners simply feel that they do not have the balance sheet strength to take risks on how the market will look 10 years from now. But while some owners may be holding back, innovation continues apace and there are now a number of technologies with a sufficiently proven track record that their future in shipping – at least for shorter routes and smaller vessel categories – looks certain. The prominent shipbroker, Clarksons, says that, including dual-fuel LNG vessels, alternative fuel ships now account for 47% of newbuild orders.[1] Several different fuel choice options are creating their own markets, each with their own advantages and drawbacks, as we shall see following consideration of the legal imperative towards a net zero shipping industry.

For many ship owners and their financial backers, maintaining the maximum potential market for their vessels at the time of onwards sale in the secondary market is a key consideration as they place orders for newbuild tonnage today.

2. International Maritime Organization

2.1 MARPOL

The International Maritime Organization (IMO) has been concerned with pollution and the protection of the marine environment, and the creation of international instruments to enforce compliance of minimum standards, since the International Convention for the Prevention of Pollution from Ships (MARPOL) was adopted in November 1973. The convention is enhanced and updated with the addition of a series of technical annexes in relation to specific subject matter, Annex VI of MARPOL[2] relates to the Prevention of Air Pollution from Ships, which entered into force in May 2005. This annex established limits for sulphur oxide and nitrogen oxide emissions from vessels and forbids the deliberate emission of ozone depleting substances – but as such is not directly concerned with carbon reduction. In 2011, amendments were made to Annex VI that enacted mandatory technical and operational energy efficiency measures for ships, aimed at reducing GHG emissions and represented the first compulsory IMO measures in this area.[3] These amendments created a new Chapter 4 to Annex VI, that entered into force in January 2013 and created an International Energy Efficiency Certificate for issue by the Flag State to vessels of over 400 gross tonnes that comply with the requirements of that Chapter. This requires ship owners to create maintain an operational Ship Energy Efficiency Management Plan (SEEMP) for their vessels and for newbuildings to establish their Energy Efficiency Design Index (EEDI) for approval by the Flag State in accordance with the technical regulations annexed to Chapter 4.

2.2 Marine Environment Protection Committee

The group within IMO tasked with advancing the carbon reduction imperative is the Marine Environment Protection Committee (MEPC). The MEPC has been working on the climate change obligation since 1997. The initial IMO Strategy on Reduction of Greenhouse Gas Emissions from Ships,[4] adopted in May 2018, aims to align international shipping with the temperature target of the Paris Agreement signed at COP21 in 2015. That strategy aims to reduce carbon intensity of international shipping by 40% by 2030, measured against a 2008 baseline, and expressly anticipates that the initial strategy shall be kept under periodic review and shall be revised and reissued in 2023. The stated vision of the initial strategy is to reduce GHG emissions from international shipping and "as a matter of urgency, aims to phase them out as soon as possible in this century".[5]

2.3 Revised strategy: MEPC 80

In July 2023, the 80th session of MEPC adopted a revised GHG policy that establishes specific reduction targets for the sector. Like the Chapter 4 amendments to MARPOL Annex VI, it contains both technical and economic measures to be developed towards the phasing out of GHG emissions. In his June 2023 address to the Working Group preparatory to MEPC 80, IMO Secretary-General Kitak Lim describes "increasing the level of ambition for 2050 and establish the intermediate check points by 2030 and 2040 that will pave the way to meet the revised vision while duly considering the impact and needs of developing states".[6] Notably, the Secretary-General concludes that "2023 is IMO's year of decisive climate action".

This development, referred to as the '2023 IMO Strategy on Reduction of GHG Emissions from Ships' is described as "enhanced common ambition to reach net zero GHG emissions from international shipping by or around ... 2050, a commitment to ensure an uptake of alternative zero and near zero GHG fuels by 2030, as well as indicative check-points for 2030 and 2040".[7] The checkpoints referred to, as a key barometer of progress, are to reduce the total annual GHG emissions from international shipping by at least 20%, striving for 30%, by 2030; and by at least 70%, striving for 80%, by 2040, each as compared to 2008.

3. UK measures

3.1 Clean Maritime Plan

In July 2019, the UK government published the Clean Maritime Plan,[8] described as an 'environment road map' and action plan towards the Maritime 2050 policy statement issued some months earlier. In the words of the Clean Maritime Plan, the vision at that time was that the UK would capture a significant share of the economic, environmental and health benefits associated with the transition to zero emission ships. This document articulates the key ambitions of the Maritime 2050 policy, including that by 2025 all vessels operating in UK waters are maximising the use of energy efficiency options and that all new vessels being ordered for use in UK waters are being designed with zero emission propulsion capability. One additional ambition is that by that time, zero emission commercial vessels are in operation in UK waters. While the latter may be true, the former seems some considerable distance from being achieved. By July 2021, this was given recognition in the government's transport decarbonisation plan,[9] which altered the ambition from the aspirational achievements for 2025 to a vaguer and less time-bound commitment. A proposed refresh of the Clean Maritime Plan in 2022 did not occur as had been originally envisaged. In September 2023, the UK government announced a new package of clean maritime measures, through the International Green Corridor Fund.

3.2 Clydebank Declaration

At COP26 in Glasgow, 24 countries signed the Clydebank Declaration in November 2021.[10] Aiming to complement the MARPOL and MEPC measures, while accelerating the pace of carbon reduction strategies for shipping, the declaration envisages voluntary participation by vessel operators. The recitals to the declaration capture the multi-faceted task ahead – including the transition in the coming decade to clean maritime fuels, zero emission vessels, alternative propulsion systems and the global availability of landside infrastructure to support them. To achieve these goals, the signatories pledged to take steps to create at least six 'green corridors' or zero emission routes between ports in signatory countries – including the essential related shoreside infrastructure – by the middle of this decade.

By focusing on specific identified routes, it is hoped that the efforts to overcome the economic, political and regulatory hurdles of zero emission vessels can be concentrated to best effect. Such ports must demonstrate and support a scalable use of zero or near-zero emission vessels. The first two corridors have been announced between the ports of Los Angeles and Shanghai, and between the ports of Antwerp and Montreal. At COP27 in Sharm el Sheikh, the governments of the UK, the US, Norway and the Netherlands pledged in November 2022 to create a task force for this purpose. During COP28, the UK and the United States reiterated their support for the 'Green Shipping Challenge', the gauntlet first laid down by the Clydebank Declaration.

By focusing on specific identified routes, it is hoped that the efforts to overcome the economic, political and regulatory hurdles of zero emission vessels can be concentrated to best effect.

3.3 UK SHORE

In March 2022, the UK government announced the creation of a new unit known as the Shipping Office for Reducing Emissions (UK SHORE) housed in the Department for Transport (DfT). Following the government's Clean Maritime Demonstration Competition (CMDC) launched in 2021, the UK SHORE aims to enhance and extend that programme of research and development of green vessel technologies and to provide funding for the shoreside infrastructure required. A fund of £206 million was created to accelerate research into new technologies and to support new skilled jobs in the sector, designed to be complementary to the National Shipbuilding Strategy.[11] The second round of CMDC aims to fund feasibility studies and trials of clean technologies towards the creation of full-scale demonstrators of their concept. UK SHORE is also the means of implementing the Clydebank Declaration green corridors initiative, subdivided into two categories: (i) international and non-ferry traffic; and (ii) domestic ferry traffic. The zero emission domestic ferries segment aims to create regional rather than international corridors, where shorter voyage distances seem most suitable to develop already existing technologies such as battery powered vessels, into greater adoption and scale.

4. Emissions trading schemes

4.1 UK

Following the transport decarbonisation plan published in 2021,[12] the UK government is consulting with industry stakeholders on proposals to include domestic maritime traffic as part of the UK Emissions Trading Scheme (ETS).[13] The leading method for doing so aims to capture shipping activity regardless of fuel source, based on vessel activity. The owner or operator of the vessel would be required to determine the volume of fuel used in each qualifying domestic journey and then multiply this by a carbon intensity factor to calculate their emissions for that voyage. Such monitoring, reporting and verification (MRV) should not be too onerous for operators of large ships who are already experienced and equipped for this – because, since January 2018, vessels calling at a European Union/European Economic Area port have been subject to the EU MRV regime; and since January 2022, ships over 5,000 gross tonnes operating on certain routes began monitoring their fuel consumption and emissions under the UK MRV regime.

It is proposed to apply the UK ETS to vessels over the same tonnage threshold, so as to allow operators of larger ships to use the MRV data to plan better and introduce efficiencies. The government believes that this lead option is likely to capture the highest quantity of emissions and that the risk of carbon leakage is low. In July 2023, the UK government published its response to the 2022 consultation process and confirmed that the scheme would include domestic maritime transport from 2026. In other words, international voyages shall remain subject to the MEPC programme of measures, while domestic journeys will require to comply with UK ETS.

4.2 EU

In July 2021, the European Commission published a series of initiatives to reduce net GHG emissions by at least 55% by 2030, against a 1990 baseline. These proposals included the extension of the EU ETS to the shipping sector; increasing demand for carbon-neural fuels; building shoreside infrastructure for alternative fuel type. In April 2023, the European Parliament formally approved the inclusion of the shipping sector within the EU ETS, with effect from 1 January 2024 for vessels of greater than 5,000 gross tonnes and transporting cargo or passengers for profit. The EU ETS will apply to 100% of emissions for voyages between two EU ports, and 50% of the emissions for voyages in which begin or end at a port in an EU member state and will be reported and verified through the existing MRV system. From 2026, the MRV regulations shall be extended to include reporting of methane and nitrous oxide in addition to carbon dioxide (CO2).

5. Low emission technologies

5.1 Electric batteries and hybrid solutions

Just as governments seek to turn widespread usage from diesel fuels toward electric battery technology for cars, trams and buses – the electrification of shipping is a live topic across the maritime sector. Advances in the battery technology available to ship owners and operators make running vessels on electricity a genuine option for some voyages. The existing general availability of shore power for recharging and the potential to use green or renewable source electricity make battery applications a near certainty for routes and vessels that are able to take advantage of the technology.

Similar to cars and much other technology running on this power application, there are limiting factors. And as with cars, the key limitation is battery capacity and endurance – the energy density of the battery required to power the tonnage and operating payload of a particular vessel, and the length of time the vessel requires to be at sea. Longer journeys can simply become unviable, and no owner will want to risk running out of power away from the shore without the means to recharge. In addition, the cost of batteries can be prohibitively high for many vessel operators.

Successful use of battery technology is already powering some pleasure boats and small ferries, particularly suited to the technology as they generally sail shorter distances and can therefore use smaller batteries. Similarly, passenger and vehicle ferries often operate between fixed and reliable ports, where the charging infrastructure can be designed around the service. These charging systems will often require taking account of the tidal range of that port and of the movement of the particular vessel. In these cases, the best fit and location of the charging system can be matched with the vessel for maximum efficiency. In Scotland, Caledonian Maritime Assets Limited pioneered the world's first seagoing diesel-electric hybrid ro-ro ferry, MV *Hallaig* in 2012. The Bavarian Lake Navigation Service run 18 electric vessels across Lake Konigssee on the German–Austrian border. The vessels move cleanly and almost noiselessly in the environmentally sensitive waters and return to their boat houses for charging. In Northern Ireland, with their MV *Pioneer* demonstrator that is now in early commercial production, Artemis Technologies have developed an all-electric zero emission hydrofoil vessel concept to be used for offshore wind crew transfer applications and tourist water taxis.

For small vessels, short crossings and similar applications with a required fuel endurance appropriate to the existing modest range of the technology, the battery solution seems ideal. However, what net zero requires of the shipping industry at large to address is the bigger

China had the first electric cargo vessel, operating on inland waterways and powered by lithium-ion batteries weighing 26 tonnes and limited to a range of just 80 kilometres.

challenges: ocean passages of very large bulk cargoes and intercontinental container traffic. In general, the currently available batteries are not sufficiently powered or are too heavy for ships that travel long distances on the high seas. China had the first electric cargo vessel, operating on inland waterways and powered by lithium-ion batteries weighing 26 tonnes and limited to a range of just 80 kilometres. More recently, the MV *Yara Birkeland* became the first fully electric autonomous cargo ship when she was launched in 2021. At 80 metres length and 3,200 tonnes the vessel is smaller than many of the cargo ships operating today (and notably below the ETS threshold of 5,000 gigatonnes) but will be capable of loading and unloading 120 containers of fertiliser for Yara, her Norwegian owners, and replace diesel truck journeys by road.

Despite the drawbacks, more electric cargo ships are expected in the coming years and the global market estimated to be valued at $16.2 billion by 2030.[14] Dutch company, Port-Liner, are building fully electric cargo ships that will operate in the Netherlands and Belgium, including out of the key hub port at Rotterdam. In the meantime, hybrid technology can meet some of the demand for more fuel-efficient new buildings. Many vessels of medium scale up to and including bulk carriers, already use diesel engines that charge electric batteries which, in turn, drive the propeller, resulting in an efficiency saving and lower hydrocarbon fuel use. These batteries can also be charged from other sources. To this end Maersk has announced that it will install offshore charging stations that will allow its vessels to recharge while waiting outside some ports. The hybrid passenger ship, MV *Vision of the Fjords*, charges its batteries from surplus energy generated by a diesel engine and also from shore power when docked. The ship can run from battery power alone for three hours when touring the Norwegian fjords. We are likely to see more of this flexibility in vessels in the immediate future.

5.2 Hydrogen

In the search for new zero emission fuel types, the hydrogen-powered revolution is eagerly anticipated, and ship owners are taking close note as more hydrogen ship concepts and designs are coming to market. As yet, there are no hydrogen-fuelled seagoing cargo ships, but the concept is nonetheless one of the most discussed likely fuels of the future for the maritime industry. The world's first hydrogen-powered inland waterways dry cargo vessel, MV *Antonie*, was constructed at Concordia Damen in the Netherlands, with sea-trials planned in late 2023 for her owner, inland shipping company, Lenten Scheepvaart.

The hydrogen fuel technology works by using hydrogen drawn from storage cylinders onboard the vessel as a source of energy to drive an electric motor. Produced through electrolysis, the only emission from the process is water vapour, with zero carbon emissions. The key drawback is not that technology, it is the hydrogen itself and the surrounding infrastructure. How the hydrogen is manufactured; how to get it to the vessel; and how and where to store it onboard – are all present challenges to an industry keen to embrace this fuel. At present, much of the hydrogen available is manufactured using fossil fuels and thus increasing the overall carbon footprint of the vessel, and so defeating the ecological benefit. However, hydrogen can be produced without recourse to fossil fuels, and it is this 'green hydrogen' that is most exciting to an industry looking to decarbonise. The process of creating the hydrogen fuel can also be carried out on board the vessel. The experimental MV *Energy Observer* project is the world's first hydrogen fuel cell ship. Launched in 2017, this catamaran design carries wind turbines and solar panels which allow it to produce its own hydrogen fuel using electrolysis of salt water. In this way, hydrogen fuel systems can be successfully combined with alternative energy sources, creating options for the power needed to carry out the electrolysis.

While the MV *Energy Observer* gives a positive vision of the future, it should be noted that none of this technology is yet economical: so far hydrogen ships are proving to be on average twice as expensive as vessels using conventional hydrocarbon fuel types. Further, scalability is everything when it comes to meeting the commercial needs of global trade routes. The shipping industry needs big solutions to meaningfully replace the current volume of marine diesel consumed. For hydrogen applications, like all new technologies under consideration, shore-side infrastructure is also fundamental to likely long-term success. While at a prototype stage, on-board manufacture of hydrogen appears an attractive solution in theory, but focus is also needed on how to ensure reliable bunkering of pre-produced hydrogen, and storage of that hydrogen onboard. The development of appropriate port facilities and concerns such as the safe storage and transportation of a product that is highly flammable will all influence ship owners' ongoing decisions about placing newbuild orders using this choice of fuel. While no large commercial application is yet in existence for this fuel type, significant investment in such shoreside facilities appears distant in time when compared to the urgency of the zero emission imperative.

5.3 Ammonia

Certain of the issues around the storage and transportation of hydrogen can be resolved by converting the hydrogen into ammonia. Plans for ammonia-powered vessels are well developed, although there are no commercial applications of this fuel type yet in operation. Ammonia demands significantly less storage room than hydrogen and does not require carefully controlled environmental factors that

The development of appropriate port facilities and concerns such as the safe storage and transportation of a product that is highly flammable will all influence ship owners' ongoing decisions about placing newbuild orders using this choice of fuel.

mitigate some of the volatility of hydrogen. Ammonia also has a higher density, generating more energy appropriate to larger vessels that travel longer distances. Accordingly, while hydrogen may be suitable for vessels where higher speeds or shorter voyages are in contemplation, significant predictions are being made for the future use of ammonia as a potential fuel for the largest intercontinental cargo ships.

There are various projects underway to make ammonia as fuel a reality for the maritime sector including design concepts for Norwegian offshore support vessels, one of which will have an ammonia-burning engine, and another will have an ammonia-powered fuel cell. In another project, a New York harbour tug is being retrofitted with an ammonia-to-power engine and planned for service in late 2023. In August 2023, the passenger ferry, MV *Sea Change*, took its maiden voyage across the Bay of San Francisco, powered solely by hydrogen. In November 2023, Yara International announced the world's first container ship that will use clean ammonia as fuel, for routes between Norway and Germany.

As with hydrogen, ammonia does not emit CO_2 but its production is conventionally powered by fossil fuels, impacting the purpose of reducing GHG emissions. Ammonia can be made with renewable

The marine industry still needs to reassure itself and others that strict standards and training for dealing with ammonia at sea and ashore will be in place.

energy (referred to as green ammonia) resulting in zero emissions from 'well to wake' and significant effort is being made to expand production of that kind. However, the supply of green ammonia does remain limited. Ammonia is already used to make fertiliser, plastics and cleaning products, and competition from other sectors for this carbon-neutral ammonia is expected to keep prices high.

More positively, because ammonia is already a widely used and traded commodity, the global infrastructure needed for the successful distribution and storage is therefore already well established, including availability at 130 ports worldwide. This is a significant early advantage in the race for secured bunkering among the competing new fuel types. For this reason, shipping companies are taking ammonia seriously: engine manufacturing giant Wärtsilä has a proven engine concept running on 70% ammonia and expect to have a pure ammonia marine combustion engine by the close of 2023. Equinor are developing an offshore supply vessel, MV *Viking Energy*, which currently runs on liquefied natural gas, to be converted to green ammonia as fuel, supplied by a plant in southern Norway. Nonetheless, the marine industry still needs to reassure itself and others that strict standards and training for dealing with ammonia at sea and ashore will be in place. Ammonia is highly toxic, flammable and corrosive. In case of accident and leakage it presents a serious risk for human and aquatic life.

5.4 Liquified natural gas

In contrast to the nascent development of hydrogen and ammonia applications, with an estimated 200 existing vessels in service and a further 250 on order, liquified natural gas (LNG) is an established alternative to marine diesel. LNG bunkering is already available in most major shipping hubs, and the infrastructure continues to improve. On the ship owner side, demand for LNG technology, especially in newbuildings has been strong due to a combination of proven track record of technology and design, environmental benefits and energy efficiency.

LNG is cooled to a liquified state and stored in cryogenic form. It produces 40% less CO2 than coal and 30% less than fuel oil and minimises the emissions of other particulates such as sulphur dioxide and mercury. It is affordable and is considered by many to be a 'transition fuel' for the shipping industry to make its way to net zero without asking investors to take chances on undeveloped and novel technology. It is cheaper than many future fuels such as hydrogen and some of the on-market biofuels, but recent LNG price rises have impacted vessel owners. Regrettably, LNG remains a fossil fuel, with an ultimately limited supply. LNG has a high methane content and while the use of LNG offsets GHG emissions, the emissions deriving from unburned methane from engines (known as methane slip) can compromise that positive reduction. While LNG applications can be said to lower emissions as compared to the current GHG output of the shipping industry, many feel that encouraging LNG use is at odds with the ambitions of the net zero imperative. Indeed, uptake of LNG technology may inhibit the adoption of technologies running on other cleaner energy sources. Some have argued that between the methane emissions and the carbon footprint LNG supply chain, this fuel type is working against progress by shifting shipping from one fossil fuel to another.

Despite this, the LNG option is growing in popularity and a quarter of EU vessels are expected to be LNG-powered by 2030. According to Marine Insight, the 2022 cumulative value of LNG newbuilding orders was US$33,742 million, an increase of 87% on the year before, including an order for 19 such vessels placed by the conglomerate MOL.[15] This has been described as an unprecedented demand but it remains to be seen whether this continues at the same rate. In a 2021 commentary by McKinsey, the authors warn that while LNG appears resilient in the near future, "LNG will ultimately be substituted by renewable energy sources or undergo emissions mitigation".[16] The same report predicts that LNG fuel demand will grow until the mid-2030s but will then decline. For now, LNG is cleaner than diesel, but as we move forward it is unlikely to be considered clean enough.

5.5 Biofuels

Biofuels work in a similar way to conventional marine diesel but are produced from renewable sources converted into liquid fuel. There are various origins and blends of biofuel, including those based on sources such as used vegetable oil, animal fats and those made from plant materials. Ethanol, biodiesel and renewable hydrocarbon fuels all fall into this category. The last of these acts as ready ‘drop in’ fuels – that is to say that they can replace petroleum-based fuels and hence lower emissions without a significant change to existing on-board machinery or portside infrastructure. Biofuels generally benefit from being easy to handle and to store, and for this reason are compatible with many existing shore facilities and existing standard vessel designs. They can be blended into fossil fuels to ‘green’ those fuels, acting in a familiar way that requires little by the way of training or technology for those crewing the vessel.

All of this makes biofuel a popular choice for ship owners looking to decarbonise. Singapore reported that biofuels outsold LNG in 2022 and various of the large players in the industry are upping their biofuel fleet as well as contributing to research on best practice. CMA CGM have increased the adoption of their biofuel fleet in conjunction with the Maritime and Port Authority of Singapore. This involves a trial of

Biofuels generally benefit from being easy to handle and to store, and for this reason are compatible with many existing shore facilities and existing standard vessel designs.

various blends of biofuels on 32 different container ships and reviewing the results and emissions. The story of the types of blends is very much a developing one: different blends are taking on a regional quality with, for example, EU and Singapore at present prefer different product types. Harmonisation is expected to follow more research and greater availability of operational data. Some of the downsides that researchers are trying to mitigate involve the impact of the biofuels on the machinery they are serving. Microbial growth, corrosion and the degradation of rubber sealings, gaskets and hoses have all been reported as side effects of the use of this type of product. Further, there is a need to provide transparency in the supply chain so that owners and operators can more fully understand the nature of what they are putting into their engines.

Methanol, like ethanol, is sometimes referred to as a biofuel and sometimes treated as a category part. It is a water-soluble and readily biodegradable, clean burning fuel that is increasingly attractive for use in the marine sector. Methanol is less toxic to aquatic life than traditional hydrocarbon fuels. It can be produced with natural gas but has versatile and mature production pathways including being made from sewage, municipal solid waste and agricultural waste. Sustainably sourced methanol can also be used as a 'drop in' fuel to lower overall emission and carbon footprint on vessel voyages in combination with conventional marine gas oil, or can be used alone.

In 2015, Stena Line of Norway converted the ro-pax ferry MV *Stena Germanica* to operate using both methanol and diesel, and in May 2023 announced the construction of two 'NewMax' car ferries of this fuel choice. In June 2023, Maersk confirmed the maiden voyage of a 2,100 TEU feeder ship, yet to be named, to powered by methanol between Korea and Denmark. Methanol was the second largest alternative fuel source choice for newbuildings in 2022 after LNG, and investing in methanol technology is generally viewed as low risk by the industry. By mid-2023, there were 25 methanol-powered vessels in operation, with 81 on order.

5.6 Wind propulsion

Harnessing the power of sail might be thought a backwards step for the shipping industry, but wind is being revisited by marine and power engineers around the world as an alternative energy source for commercial vessels. A variety of wind-powered technology is in development or already in active service. The advantages of making use of this technology are obvious: wind is free and in plentiful (if unpredictable) supply across the world's oceans – and is as green as can be, with zero emissions, no significant supply chain carbon footprint or issues with shoreside bunkering infrastructure and availability. The technology is not universally suitable for all vessels, routes or weather conditions. However, a small commercial fleet of around 20 vessels is already being supported by this technology.

Energy can be generated to power the vessel using a variety of wingsail, kitesail or fixed rotors. This energy can then support the vessel's power needs, providing anywhere from between 10% and 90% depending on the wind, the technology and particular requirements of the vessel at any time. Often the technology can be retrofitted to existing vessels and contribute to an energy efficiency of up to 20% while maintaining the existing engine apparatus, but with corresponding reduction in emissions. It is not, however, plain sailing. Wind presents particular challenges for larger tonnage, including size of the sail required and its influence on the stability of the vessel, and the ability of the crew to manipulate the wind into a safe and useable power source. To a certain extent this can be mitigated by computer management of the systems. The container ship MV *Onego Deusto*, launched in 2007 for owners Beluga Shipping GmbH and with a carrying capacity of 474 TEU, was the first vessel to be co-powered by a computer-controlled kite rig in addition to marine gas oil. This 'SkySails' system involves a kite attached to the vessel of some 320m^2, acting as an auxiliary power source, and reducing fuel consumption by around 10%.

The development and adoption of cleaner propulsion technologies, such as alternative fuels, electric propulsion and hydrogen fuel cells offer promising solutions to reduce GHG emissions and promote a greener shipping industry.

In October 2022, the MV *Shofu Maru*, a bulk carrier went into operation as part of the Mitsui OSK Lines fleet. She is the world's first cargo ship equipped with 'Wind Challenger', a hard-sail propulsion system, which uses a telescopic sail to generate power. The gains are modest – the system is expected to reduce power consumption by around 5% on sailings between Japan and Australia. Ironically, the new vessel will be dedicated to the shipment of fossil fuel, transporting coal from Newcastle, New South Wales.

6. Conclusion

In conclusion, the implementation of greener propulsion technologies in shipping is crucial for meeting global net zero targets by 2050. As the demand for maritime transportation continues to grow, it is imperative that we prioritise sustainable practices to minimise the industry's environmental impact. The development and adoption of cleaner propulsion technologies, such as alternative fuels, electric propulsion and hydrogen fuel cells offer promising solutions to reduce GHG emissions and promote a greener shipping industry. There is no clear front-running technology. It will depend on the route, weather conditions, size of vessel. No one-size-fits-all, but a combination of various greener propulsion technologies will help to reduce the GHG emissions generated by conventional fuel types. This does not make it easy for investors to choose which technology to back and there is a risk that the *status quo* will prevail for too long for net zero targets to be met.

The industry must contend with the potentially significant costs of converting vessels or building new, but with concerted efforts from stakeholders, policymakers and industry leaders, we can pave the way for a sustainable future in shipping, contributing to the global goal of achieving net zero emissions.

Notes

1 Jasmina Ovcina Mandra, "Clarksons says alternative fuel ships account for 47 pct of orderbook, project another 100 LNG carrier orders", Offshore Energy, 31 March 2023, www.offshore-energy.biz/clarksons-says-alternative-fuel-ships-account-for-47-pct-of-orderbook-projects-another-100-lng-carrier-orders.
2 See https://media.liscr.com/marketing/liscr/media/liscr/online%20library/maritime/res%20mepc.328
(76)%20-%202021%20revised%20marpol%20annex%20vi.pdf.
3 Resolution MEPC.203(62), https://imorules.com/MEPCRES_203.62.html.
4 Resolution MEPC.304(72), www.cdn.imo.org/localresources/en/KnowledgeCentre/IndexofIMOResolutions/MEPCDocuments/MEPC.304(72).pdf.
5 International Maritime Organization (IMO), "Initial IMO GHG Strategy", www.imo.org/en/MediaCentre/HotTopics/Pages/Reducing-greenhouse-gas-emissions-from-ships.aspx#:~:text=IMO%20remains%20committed%20to%20reducing,as%20possible%20in%20this%20century.
6 Opening Remarks, Intersessional Working Group on Reduction of GHG Emissions from Ships (ISWG-GHG 15), 26 June 2023, www.imo.org/en/MediaCentre/SecretaryGeneral/Pages/Intersessional-Working-Group-on-Reduction-of-GHG-Emissions-from-Ships-(ISWG-GHG-15)-.aspx#:~:text=It%20is%20now%20time%20to,and%20needs%20of%20developing%20States.
7 IMO Press Release, 7 July 2023, www.imo.org/en/MediaCentre/HotTopics/Pages/Cutting-GHG-emissions.aspx#:~:text=The%20revised%20IMO%20GHG%20Strategy%20includes%20an%20

enhanced%20common%20ambition,shipping%20to%20reach%20net%2Dzero.
8 Department for Transport (DfT), "Clean Maritime Plan", July 2019, https://assets.publishing.service.gov.uk/media/5d24a96fe5274a2f9d175693/clean-maritime-plan.pdf.
9 DfT, "Decarbonising Transport: A Better, Greener Britain", 2021, https://assets.publishing.service.gov.uk/media/610d63ffe90e0706d92fa282/decarbonising-transport-a-better-greener-britain.pdf.
10 GOV.UK, Policy Paper, "COP26: Clydebank Declaration for green shipping corridors", updated 6 December 2023, www.gov.uk/government/publications/cop-26-clydebank-declaration-for-green-shipping-corridors/cop-26-clydebank-declaration-for-green-shipping-corridors.
11 See Ministry of Defence, "National Shipbuilding Strategy – Fact Sheet", https://assets.publishing.service.gov.uk/media/5a81fdb440f0b62305b91e5b/04092017a_NSBS_Factsheet.pdf.
12 See n 9 above.
13 GOV.UK, Policy Paper, "UK Emissions Trading Scheme markets", updated 2 January 2024, www.gov.uk/government/publications/uk-emissions-trading-scheme-markets/uk-emissions-trading-scheme-markets.
14 PR Newswire, "Electric ship market worth $16.2 billion by 2030", 11 October 2021, www.prnewswire.co.uk/news-releases/electric-ship-market-worth-16-2-billion-by-2030-exclusive-report-by-marketsandmarkets-tm—857408433.html.
15 Jasmina Ovcina Mandra, "VV: 2022 saw over 160 LNG carriers order, with Japanese owners leading the pack", Offshore Energy, 27 December 2022, www.offshore-energy.biz/vv-2022-saw-over-160-lng-carriers-ordered-with-japanese-owners-leading-the-pack/#:~:text=The%20value%20of%20LNG%20newbuilding,Shipping%2C%20with%2044%20contracts%20inked.
16 McKinsey & Company, "The impact of decarbonization on the gas and LNG industry", 30 June 2021, www.mckinsey.com/industries/oil-and-gas/our-insights/the-impact-of-decarbonization-on-the-gas-and-lng-industry.

VII. Aviation and the jet zero ambition

Anna Ai
Sophie Black
Sheyda Rimmer
Addleshaw Goddard

1. Introduction

Aviation stakeholders throughout the United Kingdom and many other countries are: (i) developing, testing and using new low carbon technologies; (ii) promoting the use of zero carbon and alternative hydrocarbon aviation fuels; and (iii) implementing operational efficiencies; to achieve net zero by 2050 in line with the goals of the Paris Agreement[1] and (in the UK) the Climate Change Act 2008.

Governments, industry regulators, technology providers, airlines, airports and their suppliers all have roles to play in decarbonising aviation. Driving change is a mixture of mandatory, self-imposed and government-recommended environmental targets, policies, law and aviation regulation (outlined below) as well as consumer demand.

Meeting environmental targets – against the backdrop of forecasts that air traffic will continue to grow over the next 20 years – will pose challenges in respect of: (i) financial resource; (ii) technology risk; (iii) sourcing new aircraft fuel; (iv) regulatory approval; (v) airport infrastructure; (vi) airspace congestion; (vii) lack of worldwide environmental policy; (viii) integration with other transport modes; and (ix) community engagement. The UK recognises the importance of decarbonising the aviation sector to meet its net zero target by 2050, which it acknowledged as "hugely challenging" in the UK government's Jet Zero Strategy.[2]

In this chapter, we consider the legal, political and regulatory background to sustainable aviation (primarily from the perspective of the UK) and how the aviation industry may look like in the future. To conclude, we summarise some of the key challenges the aviation industry will face and some solutions to those challenges which are being considered and/or implemented by industry stakeholders around the world.

2. Legal, political and regulatory background to sustainable aviation

International governments, lawmakers and regulators have an important role in the future of sustainable aviation to harmonise standards, policies, laws and incentives so that a global approach is taken to new technologies and fuel sources. Airlines will require compatible sustainable fuels at all airports they operate from (including contingency airports); aircraft manufacturers will require assurance that new technologies are capable of safety clearance by regulators in other countries; and investors require certainty of demand.

Worldwide, many aviation laws and policies are already aligned to ensure a consistent approach is taken to safety and security. The International Civil Aviation Organization (ICAO) was formed as a United Nations agency in 1947 to serve as the global forum for international civil aviation and to work with member states to coordinate aviation regulation and procedures worldwide. More recently, the ICAO has increasingly focused on state action plans and global goals to achieve a sustainable aviation industry.

In the UK, most airlines and airports are independent of the government and state ownership, save for some local authority owned (or partly owned) airports. Regulation of UK airspace and aviation is carried out by the Department for Transport (DfT) and the Civil Aviation Authority (CAA), a statutory public corporation.

This chapter summarises: (i) the legal and political background to sustainable aviation in the UK; (ii) the role of the regulator in driving change and innovation; (iii) how airspace modernisation can impact carbon emissions; and (iv) other government interventions.

2.1 Key sustainable aviation policies and legislation

The UK has developed a range of domestic policies, initiatives and regulations aimed at reducing aviation emissions. There are also regional and international regulatory frameworks that are relevant to the UK, which provide a platform for harmonising standards and facilitating international collaboration. The key domestic, regional and international policies and legal instruments relevant to the UK's aviation emissions are outlined below in chronological order:

The UK has developed a range of domestic policies, initiatives and regulations aimed at reducing aviation emissions. There are also regional and international regulatory frameworks that are relevant to the UK, which provide a platform for harmonising standards and facilitating international collaboration.

(a) Convention on International Civil Aviation

Signed in 1944, the Convention on Civil Aviation (the 'Chicago Convention')[3] established ICAO and is continuously updated to reflect modern aviation practices, including international aviation environmental standards.

(b) Environmental Protection Act 1990 and other non-aviation specific environmental legislation

In common with other businesses in the UK, aviation stakeholders must meet statutory requirements regarding waste, water quality and environmental protection.

(c) Civil Aviation Act 2012

This obliges: (i) the CAA to publish information relating to the environmental effects of civil aviation in the UK; and (ii) the CAA and secretary of state, when carrying out their functions under the act, to secure that operators of licenced airports take reasonable measures to reduce, control or mitigate the adverse environmental effects (including emissions and noise) of those airports.

(d) Paris Agreement[4]

This is a legally binding international treaty on climate change adopted in Paris in 2015. It contains a commitment from the parties to the agreement to pursue efforts to limit the increase in the global average temperature to 1.5°C above pre-industrial levels.

(e) Carbon Offsetting and Reduction Scheme for International Civil Aviation (CORSIA)[5]

A global carbon reporting and offsetting scheme introduced in 2016 by the ICAO. A baseline level of carbon dioxide (CO_2) emissions is established for aircraft operators undertaking international flights, and airline operators buy and surrender emission units representing CO_2 emission reductions generated by non-aviation projects in other sectors. Aircraft operators must monitor and report emissions each year. The scheme is voluntary for all ICAO member countries until 2026 during the pilot and first phases and mandatory for all member countries from 2027. Least developed countries, small island developing states, landlocked developing countries and states that have a very small share of international traffic will not be required to participate in the mandatory stage, unless they volunteer to participate in it.

(f) IATA 2050 Commitment[6]

Airline members of the International Air Transport Association (IATA) and aviation industry bodies pledged in 2021 to achieve goals aimed at achieving net zero emissions by 2050. This represented an improvement in the previous emissions goal of the members largely due to improvements in fuel efficiency and aircraft design.

(g) Air Navigation (Carbon Offsetting and Reduction Scheme for International Aviation) Order 2021[7]

This statutory instrument implements the monitoring, reporting and verification requirements of CORSIA in the UK.

(h) Sixth Carbon Budget (Climate Change Act 2008 and Carbon Budget Order 2021[8])

This sets a legally binding UK government five-year cap on emissions from 2033–2037 and, for the first time, includes emissions from international aviation.

(i) Air Traffic Management and Unmanned Aircraft Act 2021

This Act gives the secretary of state powers to direct – for the first time – air navigation service providers and airports to progress or cooperate in airspace change proposals, and the CAA powers to impose penalties for failures to comply with such directions.

(j) UK Emissions Trading Scheme (UK ETS)

The UK ETS, effected through the Greenhouse Gas Emissions Trading Scheme Order 2020,[9] is a cap-and-trade CO_2 emissions scheme which applies to energy intensive industries and aviation. It caps how much CO_2 can be emitted and decreases the amount each year. Most aircraft operators departing from the UK and arriving in the UK or a European Economic Area (EEA) state are required to report emissions and surrender allowances equal to their emissions. Allowances can be received, bought or traded. The UK ETS came into force in 2021 to replace the UK's participation in the EU ETS (the EU-wide equivalent scheme). On 3 July 2023, the UK Emissions Trading Scheme Authority confirmed[10] that the free allocation for the aviation sector will be phased out for the 2026–2030 allocation period. To allow time for businesses to prepare, aircraft operators will receive their existing entitlement for the 2024 and 2025 scheme years and free allocation entitlement will reduce at the existing fixed amount of 2.2% annually in 2024 and 2025, until full auctioning in 2026.

(k) Jet Zero Strategy (domestic)[11]

The Jet Zero Strategy is a UK government plan published in July 2022 for achieving net zero aviation in the UK by 2050. The plan is built upon the six core policy measures of: (i) system efficiencies (including airspace modernisation); (ii) sustainable aviation fuels (SAF) (including the launch of a £165 million Advanced Fuel Fund to support the development of SAF plants); (iii) zero emission flight (including funding technology research); (iv) markets and removals (such as ETS and CORSIA); (v) influencing consumers (working alongside the CAA); and (vi) addressing non-CO_2 emissions.

Least developed countries, small island developing states, landlocked developing countries and states that have a very small share of international traffic will not be required to participate in the mandatory stage, unless they volunteer to participate in it.

(l) UK SAF mandate[12] (due to commence 1 January 2025 pending parliamentary approval)

This is a greenhouse gas (GHG) reduction scheme, which will be implemented via a statutory instrument pursuant to the Energy Act 2004, to mandate jet fuel suppliers to supply increasing levels of jet fuel from sustainable sources (2% in 2025, 10% in 2030 and 22% in 2040) with tradeable certificates with a monetary value. The mandate will apply to all jet fuel suppliers that supply certain types of fuels with strong sustainability requirements. To deal with concerns regarding sustainability of the feedstock required to produce SAF, the UK SAF mandate will introduce a cap on the use of SAF derived from hydroprocessed esters and fatty acids (currently, the most common SAF feedstock) and a 'power to liquid fuel' obligation will be introduced from 2028 (0.2% of total jet fuel demand) to incentivise production (as whilst power to liquid is currently a more expensive way of producing SAF, there is a higher GHG emissions saving potential).

(m) EU SAF mandate (ReFuelEU)

A regulation formally adopted by the European Council on 9 October 2023.[13] It requires aircraft departing from EU airports to refuel using an at least 2% SAF blend from 1 January 2025, increasing incrementally to 70% by 2050 and is enforced by fines (implemented by the relevant EU member state) for non-compliance. It applies to aviation fuel suppliers at EU airports, aircraft operators departing from EU airports, and EU airports. The regulation creates an interdependency to ensure that the three parties collaborate effectively to meet SAF goals. This approach by the EU contrasts to the proposed UK mandate whereby the obligation will fall only on the owner of the fuel at the specified assessment time. The regulation also includes measures to prevent the practice of 'fuel tankering' by requiring aircraft operators to refuel prior to departure from airports in EU member states.

2.2 Role of the regulator in sustainable aviation

(a) UK regulator

Complementing its critical responsibilities of regulating aviation safety, security and consumer protection, the CAA has an important role to play regarding sustainable aviation including when exercising the following statutory functions under the Civil Aviation Act 1982, Transport Act 2000, Civil Aviation Act 2012, Air Navigation Directions 2023 and Air Navigation Orders, namely:

- assessing and certifying the airworthiness of new aircraft and safety of fuels. In its role as enabler of low and zero emission

aviation technology, the CAA has developed the CAA Innovation Hub/Sandbox Service for the Future Flight Challenge;[14]
- considering any adverse effects on the environment from noise or pollution when exercising any aerodrome licencing or certification function;
- developing policy on the modernisation of airspace and approving changes (described in further detail in section 2.3 below) including taking account of guidance on environmental objectives given to it by the secretary of state when deciding whether to approve an airspace change; and
- reporting on aviation industry sustainability performance, including noise.

Lastly, other UK regulators will also be involved in shaping the direction of sustainable aviation including the Health and Safety Executive in relation to the sign-off of use of alternative fuels at airports (particularly the handling of hydrogen) and the Gas and Electricity Markets Authority operated through the Office of Gas and Electricity Markets (Ofgem).

(b) Worldwide regulators

The European Union Aviation Safety Agency (EASA) regulates safety and environmental protection in civil aviation across EU member states. The Federal Aviation Administration (FAA) regulates civil aviation in the United States. While the CAA, EASA and FAA are independent regulators, they regularly enter into bilateral safety arrangements with other national aviation authorities. For example, all three regulators are working together to harmonise certification of electric vertical take-off and landing (eVTOL) aircraft.

2.3 Airspace modernisation

Since the 1950s, the design of the UK's airspace (including flight routes) has remained unchanged. After decades of increased flight numbers, technological innovations (including satellite-based navigation systems and improvements in communication), pressure from new types of aircraft (including drones, eVTOLs and spacecraft) and changes in law and policy, airspace modernisation is required.

Since 2015, the CAA and DfT have been reviewing airspace policy and regulation, culminating in three key outputs:

- The CAA has produced an Airspace Modernisation Strategy (most recently updated in January 2023)[15] which sets out the overarching delivery plan for all of the UK's airspace and includes an Environmental Sustainability Strategy as an overarching principle. The vision of the strategy is to "deliver quicker, quieter and cleaner journeys and more capacity".[16]

- The CAA has been tasked with managing the CAP1616[17] airspace change process which allows sponsors (airport operators and air navigation service providers) to develop and seek CAA approval of airspace change proposals regarding the airspace boundaries within their control. Controlled airspace is where air traffic control needs to have positive control over aircraft to maintain safe separation between aircraft both at a high level above airports and at a lower level in the control zone of each airport.
- The DfT and CAA have commissioned NATS (En Roue) plc (NERL) to create an airspace change masterplan which will coordinate the implementation of airspace changes across the UK up to 2040. Once the DfT and CAA confirm the masterplan is consistent with government policy and the CAA's regulatory functions (utilising the Airspace Change Masterplan – Assessment Framework[18] published by the CAA in June 2024), it will be accepted into the Airspace Modernisation Strategy and will form the basis against which individual airspace change decisions are made by the CAA through the CAP1616 process.

The potential benefits of the airspace change programme from an environmental perspective include:

- more direct flight routes and shorter holding patterns, reducing flight time and total emissions. The biggest airspace change implemented to date ('Free Route Airspace' over Scotland in 2021) has removed traditional air routes and allows airlines to plan optimal trajectories based on weather, enabling a reduction of 12,000 tonnes of CO2 per year. Free Route Airspace will eventually be implemented across Europe with estimates of a 20m-tonne reduction of CO2; and
- reduction in noise levels for neighbouring communities if planes take-off and/or land at different altitudes. However, if the local airspace change programme adjusts a flight route, different parts of the community may experience noise pollution to which they were not previously exposed. There is, therefore, a substantial community engagement aspect to airspace modernisation.

Progressing through the UK airspace modernisation CAP1616 process is time-consuming and expensive for airport operators – particularly as the CAP1616 guidance continues to evolve. Airport operators may also now be forced into participating in the programme, regardless of their financial situation, through a direction from the secretary of state under the Air Traffic Management and Unmanned Aircraft Act 2021.

The expense of implementing airspace modernisation is recognised by the UK government who provided £3.7 million of funding in 2022/2023 to support airports in the completion of stage 2 of their airspace change proposals.

2.4 Government interventions

Several examples of government interventions are mentioned above including: (i) the UK Emissions Trading Scheme; (ii) the Sixth Carbon Budget; (iii) the ReFuelEU Regulation (which will address the issue of 'tankering' – when airlines purchase SAF at the departing airport for both its outward and return journeys where fuel is more expensive at the destination airport (leading to extra fuel consumption)); and (iv) the Air Traffic Management and Unmanned Aircraft Act 2021 (under which the UK secretary of state has new powers to direct air navigation service providers and airports to progress or cooperate in airspace change proposals).

Other strategies that governments have used to reduce carbon emissions from aviation include the announcement by France in May 2023 of a ban on short domestic flights for journeys that take less than two-and-a-half hours by train. This may not amount to many flights but it is a tool other governments may adopt in the future, alongside other initiatives such as: (i) improving long distance train

The aviation industry is at a crossroads as trials continue to find the most effective replacement of fossil jet fuel.

services; (ii) tax increases and incentives in respect of types of fuel; and (iii) the inclusion of scope 3 emissions in carbon calculations at airports (which will include emissions from aircraft movements and surface access for airport users).

3. What does the future look like for the aviation industry?

The aviation industry is at a crossroads as trials continue to find the most effective replacement of fossil jet fuel. There are many fuel alternatives, some of which are summarised below, and it is likely that a number of options (including hybrids) will play a role in the aviation industry of the future to varying degrees. However, these should not be viewed in isolation of other initiatives to reduce aviation carbon emissions including aircraft design, retrofitting existing aircraft, airspace modernisation and airport decarbonisation projects.

3.1 Aviation fossil fuel alternatives

We are still some years off from the mass manufacture of new aircraft or large scale retrofit of existing aircraft which take advantage of alternatives to fossil jet fuel as there is still uncertainty about how future aircraft will be fuelled and what the optimum design is to increase fuel efficiency.

We are still some years off from the mass manufacture of new aircraft or large scale retrofit of existing aircraft which take advantage of alternatives to fossil jet fuel.

(a) Sustainable aviation fuel (SAF)

Studies and trials worldwide are focusing on aircraft powered by sustainable aviation fuel (SAF), green hydrogen (fuel cells or liquid form), electricity, ammonia and synthetic fuels such as e-methanol as well as hybrids with fossil jet fuel. There is much debate about the cost of fossil jet fuel alternatives, but it is generally agreed that alternative fuel sources will, in the short term, be more expensive for airlines while the technology matures and until there are economies of scale. Inevitably, this will result in increased passenger fares.

The replacement of fossil jet fuel is not just futuristic aspiration – some airports are already supplying, and some airlines are already purchasing, SAF, and many countries have implemented policies which are supporting the development and supply of SAF. In 2023, SAF represented 0.2% of global jet fuel use. SAF are renewable or waste-derived aviation fuels which meet the sustainability criteria, the key being the utilisation of feedstock the production of which does not lead to deforestation or compete with food production. Several airports are undertaking projects to pilot the use of SAF, including procurement of the fuel, adapting airport facilities for the delivery and blending of the SAF with fossil jet fuel, adjusting safety procedures and training and obtaining safety certificates from the relevant regulators.

To ensure an efficient transition to SAF (without the need for extensive aircraft and engine redesign), SAF needs to be compatible with the conventional jet fuel to substitute it. This is also important to airports as they can minimise the expense of redesigning their fuel delivery systems. The efforts are therefore focused on producing SAF as a drop-in replacement to conventional jet fuel, requiring no adaptation of engines. Such SAF is currently distributed (either continuously or in batches) by approximately 100 airports (mostly in Europe and the US).

Offtake agreements for SAF are often underpinned by investment and collaboration arrangements between the airlines and the SAF producers – to provide the much-needed capital and resources necessary to develop the production facilities and scale up the production of SAF. The offtake is the final element of such arrangements, likely to commence a few years into the future.

For example, in 2023, Wizz Air invested £5 million in Firefly Green Fuel in exchange for offtake rights for Wizz Air's UK operations from 2028, up to 525,000 tonnes over 15 years. In such forward-looking arrangements, the contractual framework must achieve the right balance between certainty of arrangements at the point of signing and flexibility required to accommodate the technical and regulatory developments in SAF production and supply, including in relation to the evolving carbon offsetting market and carbon pricing and apportioning the risk of future changes in law.

Another important area in the context of such forward-looking offtake arrangements is the quality of SAF and safety during production, transportation, storage and handling. SAF which does not meet the necessary standards or which is contaminated in the supply chain could present serious safety issues – for both aircraft and airports – and therefore potentially expose airlines to significant liabilities. Parties in the SAF supply chain can mitigate risk through contractual obligations and a chain of indemnity. The Aviation Fuel Supply Model Agreement issued by IATA[19] contains very broad indemnities to protect the airlines in the context of fuel supply, although whilst SAF is in its infancy, enforcement of indemnities may be difficult where counterparties struggle to obtain the required insurance in the market or do not have a sufficiently strong financial covenant to cover liabilities.

(b) Hydrogen

The use of SAF is not the only promising route towards decarbonisation of aviation. Airbus is aiming to develop the world's first hydrogen-powered commercial aircraft by 2035. ZeroAvia have carried out several tests of their 19-seater Dornier 228 twin-engine aircraft using hydrogen fuel cell propulsion and are aiming to provide a first commercial offering of the 10–20 seat 500 NM range in 2025. Trials were conducted as part of the HyFlyer II project backed by the UK government.

The CAA's Hydrogen Challenge[20] was launched in November 2023 to understand the potential of hydrogen fuel. It brings together the regulator with academia and industry to improve the understanding of risks involved with hydrogen use in aviation, identify gaps in policies and develop net zero policies. The challenge utilises a regulatory sandbox which will support aviation fuel stakeholders as they navigate the pathway to certification of replacement fuels.

(c) Battery electric

Electric flights will be challenging in the short-term for long-haul flights given the size and weight of batteries required but are potentially feasible for domestic flights and require minimal additional airport infrastructure. Ampaire's Electric EEL has led the way as Scotland's first electric-powered aircraft, and has been testing its short-distance capability between Kirkwall Airport and the Orkney Islands.

Airbus is aiming to develop the world's first hydrogen-powered commercial aircraft by 2035.

3.2 Aircraft design

New aeroplane designs are required due to the complex technological requirements needed to power aircraft long distances with sustainable fuels, hydrogen or electricity. Not only will this be costly, but it will take many years to roll out since the expected operational life cycle of an aircraft is over 25 years and new aircraft design takes around 10 years. In the meantime, there can be significant environmental benefits from refurbishing existing aircraft and/or improving the design of engines – including engines currently in-service. For example, Rolls-Royce claim that their UltraFan demonstrator aero engine offers a 25% fuel burn improvement on the first generation of the Trent engine.

Aircraft of the future will not necessarily look like they do in the 2020s. According to McKinsey, the advanced air mobility (AAM) industry, which includes electric air taxis (such as eVTOLs, meaning electric vertical take-off and landing) and potentially, in a more distant future, self-driving drones, made "substantial progress in 2023".[21] Future air mobility aircraft will offer an alternative to a car, tube or a train commute, and will operate frequently but at reasonably short distances.

The use of AAM is not, however, without challenges. eVTOLs will require dedicated launch and landing areas – and with the flights intended to be frequent, designating such space within cities and obtaining the necessary planning consents may be problematic.

Certification for safe use will also be a paramount issue. Vertical Aerospace was the first eVTOL company in the UK to fly after receiving a test permit from the CAA, and the CAA has been supporting Apian and Skyports in demonstration trials.

3.3 Decarbonising airports

One of the most significant challenges currently facing airport operators is how to 'future-proof' airports when there is uncertainty about government policy, regulation and technology and before they fully understand the demand for alternative fuel sources.

As part of the Jet Zero Strategy, the UK government set an ambition that airport operations in England will be required to be zero emission by 2040. There is limited clarity regarding this policy as decisions are to be made concerning what emission sources should be included in the target (eg, scope 3 which would include aircraft movements and surface access) and the type and size of airport the target should apply to. Until these issues are resolved, particularly the application of scope 3 emissions, airport operators have limited certainty as to the extent to which they need to adapt their airports in time for 2040.

One of the most significant challenges currently facing airport operators is how to 'future-proof' airports when there is uncertainty about government policy, regulation and technology and before they fully understand the demand for alternative fuel sources.

While airports in EU member states are also grappling with this uncertainty, the regulatory framework around them is tightening. In order to comply with the ReFuelEU regulation, EU airports will have to take all necessary measures to ensure that their fuelling infrastructure is available and fit for SAF distribution so that aircraft operators have access to aviation fuels containing the minimum shares of SAF. This will pose a challenge during the transition phase of operating dual pipelines whilst some airlines operate on traditional fossil fuels and others on SAF.

Regardless of direct government intervention such as the two examples above, many airport operators have taken matters into their own hands in order to decarbonise their estate by setting their own zero emission targets and rolling out initiative to meet such targets including:

- prioritising environmental benefits during airspace modernisation programmes;
- the replacement of fossil-fuelled airport vehicles with electric-powered vehicles;
- the installation of electric vehicle (EV) charging points for airport and customer vehicles;
- improving surface access options to encourage a move from cars to public transport (including for example the Heathrow Express, London Luton Airport's DART shuttle and Edinburgh Airport's tram stop);
- the installation of solar PV panels on rooftops and airfields (subject to glint and glare assessments), district heat networks and other renewable energy projects; and
- commencing feasibility studies into hydrogen use and/or production.

Redeveloping airports to increase sustainability presents numerous challenges. The complex process of planning and obtaining necessary consents can be lengthy and convoluted, often involving a multitude of stakeholders with differing priorities.

Addressing the complex energy requirements of modern airports, particularly in the context of integrating green energy solutions, is another hurdle. Whilst innovative technologies like electric aircraft and renewable energy sources hold promise, they increase electricity demands and place strain on existing grids. Hydrogen and SAF production facilities are scarce and scattered geographically so are unlikely to be aligned to the location of the airports they serve. In the absence of a pipeline supply infrastructure (and no recognition of the need for additional pipelines in current UK planning policy), servicing the airports can require multiple lorries (and multiple trips). Utilising road transport can undermine carbon reduction efforts, is unlikely to be commercially efficient on a large scale and may cause planning/permitting issues if there is a large increase in road traffic between the hydrogen production plant and the airport.

A long-term solution would be to ensure there are more sustainable options available locally, including pipelines for the delivery of hydrogen and SAF. A secure supply chain (including local expertise) needs to be established to generate sufficient quantities of all components required for alternative fuel including electrolysers, fuel cells, pipelines, fuel trucks. In the meantime, airlines should ensure that their offtake arrangements provide the required flexibility for delivery modes and mitigate their risks with respect to under-deliveries and contamination.

Airport operators and ground handlers will need to be trained in the handling of alternative fuel supplies – particularly hydrogen, which is flammable, colourless, odourless, and tasteless so it may be hard to detect leaks unless specific leak detection measures are put in place. Liquid hydrogen needs to be cooled at -253°C and stored in large, insulated tanks.

There may be significant costs for airports as they adapt their facilities, some of which will be passed to airport users subject to CAA controls over the UK's largest airports. Many smaller regional airports are not profit-making but play an essential role in the local community. Without the economies of scale, adaption of these small airports to offer users a range of fuel options will be costly. In the post-Covid era as the aviation sector emerges from significant financial loss, many airports will look for alternative sources of funding for redevelopment.

Some airports may seek long-term arrangements for the purchase of fuel and/or financing of the installation of renewable energy infrastructure (giving certainty of costs over a number of years) through power purchase agreements (PPAs).

Publicly owned airports outside of the UK occasionally use the public private partnership (PPP) model to secure private finance which is repaid over many years (akin to a mortgage). Examples range from the large-scale Turks and Caicos Howard Hamilton International Airport redevelopment PPP to small-scale hydrogen production plants at European airports.

Government funding (such as the UKRI Future Flight Challenge) may assist with plugging financial gaps for introducing new green technology or conducting trials.

There may be significant costs for airports as they adapt their facilities, some of which will be passed to airport users subject to CAA controls over the UK's largest airports.

Lastly, airports may (subject to CAA oversight in the case of larger regulated airports) seek to introduce variable charges to aircraft using the airport according to carbon emissions in a similar manner to current charges for infringement of noise thresholds.

4. Conclusion

With the commencement of airlines utilising SAF, increasing government interventions to encourage stakeholders into adopting green technology, investment in the development of sustainable aviation technology and ongoing airspace modernisation, the aviation industry has already started its sustainability journey. Some of the key challenges the industry faces, and potential solutions can be summarised as follows:

- There are a wide range of viable aviation fuel sources and aircraft technologies under development and testing with no clear picture as to what aviation will look like by 2050. The capital cost of producing new aviation fuels is significant, and funders require certainty as to future demand. Likewise, airports (including some smaller unlicenced aerodromes) will need to expend capital to adapt their infrastructure for new fuel sources and to accommodate different aircraft design (eg, future AAM). Over the last decade, the UK government has increased its commitment to this sector in order to bring about some cohesion and stability by publishing its Jet Zero Strategy, launching various research and development grants and introducing the UK SAF mandate.

- The lack of international policy cohesion bears the risk of technologies and fuels being developed which cannot be utilised worldwide either because an airport lacks the infrastructure or fails to accept certain aircraft or because an aircraft does not meet the safety requirements of the national aviation regulator. Many regulators, governments and industry stakeholders recognise this issue and are working together through the ICAO. A good example of collaboration is that the CAA and EASA have aligned safety certification standards for eVTOL aircraft which will assist UK manufacturers in gaining access to the global market for eVTOL aircraft.
- Manufacturing new aircraft, especially when it involves an innovative design, takes many years and is very costly. Shorter term solutions (such as the utilisation of CORSIA, the use of SAF and implementing airspace modernisation plans) therefore need to be maximised in order to meet emission targets.
- SAF products are in short supply, are costly to manufacture and purchase, and range significantly in quality and feedstock. The hydrogen market is even less mature – there is currently limited production and no clear answer as to how it can be easily transported to airports (particularly as there is no recognition of the need for additional pipelines in current UK planning policy). Stringent safety and environmental standards need to apply to new fuels, and the market requires stability for investors. SAF development is a core part of the Jet Zero Strategy, as evidenced by the UK government's launch of its £165 million Advanced Fuel Fund to support new SAF plants. The UK SAF mandate is a further UK government intervention which will require jet fuel suppliers to supply increasing levels of jet fuel from sustainable sources by 2030. Lastly, the CAA's recently launched Hydrogen Challenge is a clear indication that the UK government considers that hydrogen remains a contender as a future aviation fuel.

These challenges demonstrate that there is no quick, easy or cost-effective answer to reducing aviation emissions. Whilst the race is on for industry stakeholders across the world to agree on the best long-term solution, short-term measures are already being taken towards meeting the ambitious 2050 target.

The authors would like to thank to Francis Tyrrell for his contributions to this report.

Notes

1 See https://unfccc.int/files/essential_background/convention/application/pdf/english_paris_agreement.pdf.
2 Department for Transport (DfT), "Jet Zero Strategy: Delivering net zero aviation by 2050", July 2022, https://assets.publishing.service.gov.uk/media/62e931d48fa8f5033896888a/jet-zero-strategy.pdf.
3 See www.icao.int/publications/Documents/7300_cons.pdf for full text.
4 See https://unfccc.int/files/essential_background/convention/application/pdf/english_paris_agreement.pdf for full text.
5 See www.icao.int/environmental-protection/CORSIA/Pages/default.aspx for full text.
6 See www.iata.org/contentassets/d13875e9ed784f75bac90f000760e998/iata-agm-resolution-on-net-zero-carbon-emissions.pdf for full text.
7 SI 2021 No 534.
8 SI 2021 No 750.
9 SI 2020 No 1265.
10 GOV.UK, Press release, "Tighter limit on industrial, power and aviation emissions, as UK leads the way to net zero", 3 July 2023, www.gov.uk/government/news/tighter-limit-on-industrial-power-and-aviation-emissions-as-uk-leads-the-way-to-net-zero.
11 Text available at https://assets.publishing.service.gov.uk/media/62e931d48fa8f5033896888a/jet-zero-strategy.pdf.
12 DfT, "Supporting the transition to Jet Zero: Creating the UK SAF Mandate: Government response to the second consultation on the SAF Mandate", April 2024, https://assets.publishing.service.gov.uk/media/662938db3b0122a378a7e722/creating-the-UK-saf-mandate-consultation-response.pdf.
13 See https://eur-lex.europa.eu/legal-content/EN/TXT/?uri=CELEX%3A02023R2405-20231031 for full text.
14 See www.caa.co.uk/publication/download/18646.
15 UK Civil Aviation Authority (CAA), "About the Strategy: Information about the Airspace Modernisation Strategy", www.caa.co.uk/commercial-industry/airspace/airspace-modernisation/airspace-modernisation-strategy/about-the-strategy/.
16 *Ibid*, p4.
17 See www.caa.co.uk/publication/download/20735.
18 See www.caa.co.uk/publication/download/19036#:~:text=in%20Chapter%202.-,The%20airspace%20change%20masterplan,modernisation%20at%20a%20system%20level for full text.
19 See full text at www.iata.org/contentassets/ebdba50e57194019930d72722413edd4/afsma-ed-5.1-july-2023f.pdf.
20 See www.caa.co.uk/our-work/innovation/hydrogen-challenge/.
21 McKinsey & Company, "Clouds or clear skies? Prospects for future air mobility", 23 January 2024, www.mckinsey.com/industries/aerospace-and-defense/our-insights/future-air-mobility-blog/clouds-or-clear-skies-prospects-for-future-air-mobility.

Addendum

On 24 July 2024, the UK government's King's Speech announced proposals to nationalise railways, introduce tap-and-go payments across the rail network, and implement a "Better Buses Bill" aimed at granting greater local control over bus services. This initiative is designed to integrate bus services more closely with other forms of public transport, potentially leading to a more unified and user-friendly ticketing system across different modes of transport in local areas.[1]

These measures reflect a strong commitment to making public transport more accessible and user-friendly. A system where passengers can simply tap and go will undoubtedly enhance the appeal of public transport, supporting a shift towards more sustainable travel habits.

However, implementation will not be without challenges. The national rail network currently grapples with immense fare complexity, with estimates suggesting there could be as many as 55 million different fare types across the UK. Finding tap-and-go payment technology that can handle this level of complexity, or even a fraction of it, could be challenging. Simplifying fares – a necessary step before any significant rollout of tap-and-go payments – will not be straightforward, even in a nationalised and centrally managed system. Previous attempts at fare reform, such as removing return or off-peak ticket options, have faced significant consumer resistance. The ability for passengers to travel from one station to over 2,500 others, with a vast array of possible routes and train companies involved, is a reality of the UK's extensive network. Implementing fare reform is likely to be politically difficult, with as many losers as winners, if the aim is to maintain existing levels of revenue.

The "Better Buses Bill" proposes greater local control over bus services – a sharp contrast with the centralised strategy for rail. There will inevitably be operational challenges in implementing a unified contactless payment system across a fragmented bus network versus a unified rail system. Integrating more modes of transport and related ticket types may exacerbate existing issues of fare complexity and the routine acceptance of ubiquitous payment methods across the transport network as a whole.

Meeting regulatory and payment network requirements will be another challenge. For example, ensuring that consumers understand the amount they are agreeing to pay when they tap their card, and managing payment risks such as chargebacks, fraud, or insufficient funds in a cardholder's bank account at the point of tapping out – there are several 'payments' issues that will need up front thought in the tap-and-go design process.

Differentiating between various classes of train seating with a tap-and-go system also needs careful consideration to maintain service quality and fare integrity. While these challenges are not insurmountable, they will require pragmatic decisions from the government and other authorities involved. It is possible that to address these risks, the government may settle on a different model of tap-and-go, with certain ticket types (eg, high value, long or multi-train journeys, or advance/return tickets) still needing to be purchased in advance. Certainly, we would expect any national tap-and-go system to be introduced incrementally, given the complexity involved.

To conclude, while the UK government's announcement of plans to nationalise railways and introduce tap-and-go payments represents a significant stride towards more convenient and sustainable public transport, there will be much work to do. Simplifying fares, managing payment risks, maintaining clarity for consumers and overcoming the inevitable range of operational and technical implementation challenges, will be crucial to realising the full potential of these reforms.

Note

1 See, for example, www.cittimagazine.co.uk/news/legislation-regulation/bills-to-overhaul-uk-rail-and-bus-services-included-in-kings-speech.html and www.thetimes.com/uk/politics/article/labour-king-speech-keir-starmer-measures-policies-mm7qkpq3n.

About the authors

Anna Ai
Managing associate, Addleshaw Goddard
anna.ai@addleshawgoddard.com

Anna Ai advises clients in the energy, aviation and utilities sectors where regulatory advice is key. She focuses on complex projects in the emerging net zero economy, including the production and supply of sustainable aviation fuels. Her clients include Wizz Air and British Airways.

Ellen Beardsworth
Managing associate, Addleshaw Goddard
ellen.beardsworth@addleshawgoddard.com

Ellen Beardsworth joined Addleshaw Goddard's infrastructure projects and energy team six years ago and has significant experience advising public and private sector clients across transactional infrastructure, utilities and energy projects, including in the regulated sectors. She regularly advises clients in varied roles in the EV market on how to adapt and support the uptake of non-combustion engines. This includes compliance with the new regulatory framework, particularly for charge points. She also has experience advising vehicle manufacturers on the transition and was a key member of the

Addleshaw Goddard team advising VW on their multi-billion-pound EV project with Ford as part of the wider strategic partnership between the entities.

Sophie Black
Legal director, Addleshaw Goddard
sophie.black@addleshawgoddard.com

With her career history including senior legal counsel at Edinburgh Airport, Sophie Black is a leader of the Addleshaw Goddard airports and aviation team and regularly advises on aviation commercial contracts and regulatory matters. Recent career highlights include advising: a shareholder on the regulatory aspects of its equity interest in a UK airport; the purchaser of an unlicenced aerodrome on their regulatory duties; a UK airport on surface access contractual issues; an investor in an aviation logistics company on UK aviation regulation; Highlands and Islands Airports in respect of phase two of their Sustainable Aviation Test Environment Project; and the Ministry of Defence on an aviation matter.

Charles Christie
Associate, Addleshaw Goddard
c.christie@aglaw.com

Charles Christie is an associate based in Addleshaw Goddard's Dubai office who supports on commercial, technology and data mandates from across the Middle East region, with a particular focus on the United Arab Emirates and Saudi Arabia markets. He routinely drafts and advises on terms and conditions, agency and distribution agreements, commercial sponsorship and partnership agreements, technology licensing and procurement, outsourcing and goods and services contracts, as well as compliance with marketing rules and digital promotional content regulation.

Charles has particular experience advising clients on data protection matters, including compliance audits and comprehensive data mapping exercises, intra-group data sharing arrangements, cross-border data transfers, data subject rights, direct marketing and cybersecurity requirements. Prior to moving to the Middle East, Charles spent several years working in London.

Paul Dight
Partner, energy and utilities, Addleshaw Goddard
paul.dight@addleshawgoddard.com

Paul Dight led the renewables sub-sector at Addleshaw Goddard for several years and is now co-head for the energy for business sub-sector and the firm's EV charging group. Paul has advised for over 15 years on renewables schemes spanning different technologies including solar, wind, AD, waste and biomass in UK and Europe, and most CfD-backed schemes including the three largest offshore wind farms in the UK. As part of the energy for business sub-sector, Paul is helping major corporates with their energy transition and decarbonisation programmes. That work includes corporate PPAs, Europe-wide energy procurement, direct wire schemes, micro-grids and rooftop solar for a number of institutional landlords, airports and manufacturers; and EV charging schemes for several local authorities, hotel groups and CPOs throughout Europe.

Paul also specialises in heat networks, advising operators, investors, landlords and connecting parties on some of the largest schemes in the UK and SAF schemes for major airlines.

Martin Fleetwood
Consultant, Addleshaw Goddard
martin.fleetwood@addleshawgoddard.com

Martin Fleetwood is an experienced regulatory and commercial contracts lawyer working in the transport sector. He has over 25 years of experience of advising both public and private clients in the rail industry in the UK and elsewhere, including train operators (both passenger and freight), rolling stock lessors and manufacturers, infrastructure managers and governmental departments. A significant part of his work is focused on regulatory issues, both helping clients understand regulatory regimes they operate in and advising on relevant regulatory issues affecting the agreements they are negotiating.

Martin's long involvement in the rail sector means that he has a very good appreciation of the various issues affecting the different players within the industry and how these issues are often interrelated. This allows him to deliver solutions which are both commercial and practical. He writes regular articles for rail industry publications as well as speaking at various conferences and seminars.

Ellie Gilbert
Associate, Addleshaw Goddard
ellie.gilbert@addleshawgoddard.com

Ellie Gilbert is an associate in the infrastructure, projects and energy department at Addleshaw Goddard in London. She has worked with clients across a number of sectors including energy, utilities, logistics and aviation. Ellie is passionate about the energy transition and has advised clients on international sustainability regulations such as the

EU ETS, renewable energy projects including solar and offshore wind farms and on the use of alternative fuels in shipping and aviation.

Jack Houselander
Managing associate, Addleshaw Goddard
jack.houselander@addleshawgoddard.com

Jack Houselander is a commercial lawyer at Addleshaw Goddard with particular experience in payments and fintech. Jack advises a range of clients and advises on a range of commercial contracts, transactions, collaboration and product development issues. He also regularly advises on legal issues arising out of payment network rules.

Nathalie Moreno
Partner, Addleshaw Goddard
nathalie.moreno@addleshawgoddard.com

Nathalie Moreno is an international technology, data privacy, cybersecurity and AI partner at Addleshaw Goddard UK. She is a well-known and trusted adviser in the global privacy and data protection world who brings 20 years of experience and extensive knowledge to clients across sectors and jurisdictions.

Nathalie's practice encompasses the full range of data protection, e-privacy and cybersecurity issues. She regularly advises on audits, cybersecurity, data governance and legal requirements in connection with the use of new technologies (AI, IoT etc) and the new UK and EU digital and data regulations, including the EU AI Act and the EU Data Act.

Nathalie has a particular focus on the technology and automotive sectors. She is able to advise on all data, IoT and AI issues generated by the crossover between the automotive and technology industries, leading to the connected car revolution and the rise of autonomous vehicles.

Sheyda Rimmer
Associate, Addleshaw Goddard
sheyda.rimmer@addleshawgoddard.com

Sheyda Rimmer joined Addleshaw Goddard in 2021 and qualified into the finance team in Edinburgh. Sheyda has experience acting for a variety of lenders and borrowers across several areas, including corporate lending and borrowing and real estate finance. Prior to joining the finance department, she was in the infrastructure, projects and energy team during her training contract where she worked on transactions across the energy and transport sectors.

Ross Sandford
Managing associate, Addleshaw Goddard
ross.sandford@addleshawgoddard.com

Ross Sandford is a managing associate in the infrastructure and projects team at Addleshaw Goddard. Ross has advised on a range of substantive matters in relation to transport and infrastructure, including advising on rail franchising, the construction and redevelopment of railway stations as well as the implementation of the European Train Control System.

Rachel Scott
Partner, Addleshaw Goddard
rachel.scott@addleshawgoddard.com

Rachel Scott is a partner in Addleshaw Goddard's transport team, with a particular focus on the rail sector. She has over 20 years' experience advising both public and private sector clients on rail infrastructure projects, network operations and concessions and rail regulatory matters, as well as various road and highway related matters and complex government contracts.

William Smith
Partner, Addleshaw Goddard
william.smith@addleshawgoddard.com

William Smith is a partner at Addleshaw Goddard dedicated to supporting clients in the energy and transport sectors on energy transition projects and efforts to reach net zero targets. While based in London, he works for clients across the UK, Europe and the Middle East.

Will has worked on some of the largest transactions in the clean transport sector including electric vehicle platform alliances (designed to commoditise the design and build electric vehicles in a bid to drive down the cost of electric vehicle manufacture and increase adoption); zero emission (hydrogen and battery) bus fleet and rail projects; and electric vehicle charging projects, as well as electricity network and renewable generation projects.

Will's passion for decarbonisation of the transport sector led to him being invited to be consulting editor of this publication, working with his colleagues at Addleshaw Goddard on the chapters contained in this Special Report.

Anna Sweeney
Principal knowledge lawyer, Addleshaw Goddard
anna.sweeney@addleshawgoddard.com

Anna Sweeney began her career as a commercial solicitor at Eversheds and has been a professional support lawyer/knowledge lawyer since 2007. She supports the infrastructure projects and energy (IPE) team and is also the sector knowledge lawyer for the energy and transport sectors at Addleshaw Goddard. She has extensive knowledge of both energy and transport regulation and keeps the team abreast of legal and market developments in these fast-moving sectors.

Anna writes regular client updates on energy, transport and infrastructure developments and has a keen professional and personal interest in decarbonisation and limiting climate change.

Euan Towers
Legal director, Addleshaw Goddard
euan.towers@addleshawgoddard.com

Euan Towers is a legal director in the corporate and commercial division of Addleshaw Goddard and a member of the payments team. Euan advises on a range of commercial contracts and payments transactions involving various payment methods. He works for banks, technology companies, payment processors and other payments industry participants, and has over six years' experience of working across the payments market.

Ed Watt
Partner, Addleshaw Goddard
ed.watt@addleshawgoddard.com

Ed Watt is head of the shipping team and is a leading shipping lawyer, specialising in sale and purchase, shipbuilding contracts and ship registration. Ed has acted in the sale or purchase and registration of more than 300 vessels. With an international practice acting for ship owners, builders and banks, Ed has led negotiations and completions in over 25 countries and is a recognised expert in dual registration in the Caspian Sea. He routinely advises owners and charterers in relation to time and voyage charterparties and bareboat structures.

Recent work includes negotiating global contracts of affreightment with major shipping lines on behalf of retail clients, charters for dry and liquid bulk cargoes on behalf of manufacturing industries and supporting newbuilding projects for floating offshore wind developments. Ed is also a consultant to the IMO Legal Committee. Ed qualified in 1999 and is the author of *Ship Registration: Law and Practice* (3rd edn, Routledge, 2018).

About Globe Law and Business

Globe Law and Business was established in 2005. From the very beginning, we set out to create legal books that are sufficiently high level to be of real use to the experienced professional, yet still accessible and easy to navigate. Most of our authors are drawn from Magic Circle and other top commercial firms, both in the United Kingdom and internationally.

Our titles are carefully produced, with the utmost attention paid to editorial, design and production processes. We hope this results in high-quality publications that are easy to read and a pleasure to own.

In 2021, we were very pleased to announce the start of a new chapter for Globe Law and Business following the acquisition of law books under the imprint Ark Publishing. Our law firm management list is now significantly expanded with many well-known and loved Ark Publishing titles.

We are also pleased to announce the launch of our online content platform, Globe Law Online, which allows for easy access across firms. Details of all titles included can be found at www.globelawonline.com. Email glo@ globelawandbusiness.com for further details and to arrange a free trial for you or your firm.

We'd very much like to hear from you with your thoughts and ideas for improving what we offer. Please do feel free to email me on sian@globelawandbusiness.com. Happy reading and thank you for your time.

Sian O'Neill
Managing director
Globe Law and Business
www.globelawandbusiness.com